THIRD EDITION

HOW TO MAKE A
LIVING
WITH YOUR
WRITING

TURN YOUR WORDS INTO
MULTIPLE STREAMS OF INCOME

Joanna Penn

How to Make a Living with Your Writing: Turn Your Words into
Multiple Streams Of Income

Third Edition

ISBN: 978-1-913321-63-5

Published by Curl Up Press

Requests to publish work from this book should be sent to:
joanna@TheCreativePenn.com

Cover and Interior Design: JD Smith

Printed by Amazon KDP Print

www.CurlUpPress.com

Dedicated to Yaro, Kris, Dean, and Orna.

For showing me the way.

Contents

Introduction

This is the best time in history to make a living with your writing!

You can reach readers online and sell your books to a global audience, as well as make money in other ways while still educating, entertaining, or inspiring your audience.

If you love to create and you're ready to learn fresh skills in a fast-changing environment, this book will give you lots of ideas on how to make money with your words. I'll explain how I make a living with my writing and share tips from other writers on how you can do it too with practical, actionable advice that you can implement for yourself.

Each chapter provides ideas you can use to research each opportunity in more detail and questions to guide your thought process. Sometimes it's just about knowing what's out there in order to find what's right for you.

This book is not a get-rich-quick scheme, and there are easier ways to make a living than with your writing. But over the last decade, I have gone from zero to a multi-six-figure annual income based on my writing and from a miserable corporate day job to happy creative entrepreneur.

Making a living is not just about money, it's also about meaning, and writing can give you both.

From corporate day job to creative entrepreneur

I'm Joanna Penn and I spent 13 years implementing Accounts Payable systems into large corporates and small/ medium companies across Europe and Asia Pacific. I have degrees in Theology and Psychology, and I certainly didn't have any experience with creative work in my early career.

Many times over those years, I wondered how I had ended up in a job that paid well but left me creatively stunted and miserable with my life. I had nothing to show for my time but the paycheck and everything I did seemed pointless as it all disappeared as the next IT project rolled out.

I tried other things on the side — an online travel itinerary website, a scuba diving charter boat business, and property investment, but none of my ideas worked out. I reached rock bottom in 2006. I hated every single day at my job and although the money was good, I knew I had to change my life.

I started reading and listening to self-help books and podcasts, and decided to write my own book while I searched for a job I loved. I published *How to Enjoy Your Job or Find a New One* in early 2008, later rewritten and re-published as *Career Change*.

Writing that first book changed my life — not because it sold many copies, but because it opened up a new world of creative possibility.

I learned about writing books and self-publishing, blogging, podcasting and social media. I shared my journey on my blog at TheCreativePenn.com and started a podcast to talk to other creatives. While the income was tiny at first and I still had my day job, I was thrilled to be selling books and products and consulting online as well as speaking professionally.

I continued writing, publishing, blogging and podcasting, and in September 2011, I left my consulting job to become a full-time author entrepreneur. In 2015, my writing income surpassed my previous career.

From those humble beginnings, The Creative Penn Limited is now a multi-six-figure company with books at its heart. I'm an award-nominated New York Times and USA Today bestselling thriller and dark fantasy author as J.F. Penn, and I also write non-fiction under Joanna Penn. I've sold books in 162 countries and 5 languages. I'm an award-winning podcaster with two shows, *The Creative Penn* and *Books and Travel*, and I'm an international professional speaker.

My business has multiple streams of income based on my writing, including books in different formats on multiple stores, online courses, affiliate income, podcast sponsorship, and Patreon, among others. Plenty of authors make money from book sales alone, but multiple streams of income provide a measure of protection against the rollercoaster of the market. I'll go into detail on all these possibilities in the chapters ahead.

But remember, it wasn't always like this.

I started out with one book, no audience, and no experience in publishing or online sales and marketing. I took action on my ideas and learned the necessary skills along the way, adapting to the changes in the market over time — and you can do it too.

What do you want to do with your life?

As I write this, the global pandemic continues to take its daily toll. Many of us have spent time in lockdown considering that life really is short and we need to make the most of the days we have left. Yes, we want to make a living, but we also want to do work that matters.

Your writing could educate, inspire, or entertain others. Your words could change someone's life. If you love to write, I hope this book will help you to make a living from it — and a life you're happy with.

Structure of the book

We'll start with first principles, the attitude and mindset you need to adopt in order to be successful.

Part 1 will take you through how to make money with books and take control of your author career, however you choose to publish.

Part 2 goes into how to make money in other ways with writing at the heart of your creative business.

The final chapter guides you through the transition and your next steps on the journey to making a living with your writing.

There are questions for you to consider and resources to take your research further at the end of every chapter. You can download the questions, appendices, and more resources at TheCreativePenn.com/makealivingdownload

There's also a Companion Workbook available in print with all the questions so you can write in that if you prefer.

Let's get into how to make a living with your writing!

* * *

Disclaimer: I am not a lawyer, accountant, or a financial advisor. This book is based on my experience and research and is not financial or legal advice. If you have specific legal and financial questions, please seek professional advice in your jurisdiction.

Note: There are affiliate links within this book to products and services that I recommend and use personally. This means that I receive a small percentage of the sale at no extra cost to you, and in some cases, you may receive a discount for using my link. I only recommend products and services that I believe are great for writers, so I hope you find them useful.

First principles

"If you imagine less, less will be what you undoubtedly deserve. Do what you love, and don't stop until you get what you love. Work as hard as you can, imagine immensities, don't compromise, and don't waste time. Start now. Not 20 years from now, not two weeks from now. Now."

Debbie Millman, *Look Both Ways: Illustrated Essays on the Intersection of Life and Design*

There are some important first principles to consider before we get into the detail and some questions that will help you to frame the rest of the book.

What is your definition of success? What will you do to achieve it?

This book is about how to make a living with your writing, so financial success is a critical aspect. But before we get started, take a minute to step back and consider your true definition of success.

What do you really want for your writing? For the book you're working on? For your author career? For your life?

If you don't know what your definition of success is, how will you know if you achieve it and how will you know what direction to take to get there?

There are a lot of ideas in this book, but you can't implement them all. You have to choose what will work for your creative path ahead, for your personality, and for your lifestyle.

Your definition of success will determine what you write, how you publish and market your books, and what kind of income streams you choose to create. For example, do you want to win a literary prize? Or do you want to make six figures in a single year from book sales? While a few rare authors can achieve these at the same time, most will have to choose between critical acclaim and significant commercial success.

You can do everything, but not at the same time, and your definition of success will inevitably change over time as you hit your goals.

When I started out in my writing career, my primary definition of success was to leave my job, then make six figures, then multi-six-figures, and now, 15 years after I started writing my first book, I'm interested in awards. Consider what's important to you and how you're going to measure success.

You also need to think about what you're willing to do to achieve your goal. Books don't write themselves, and a thriving creative business takes years to establish. We're all busy and there is never enough time — but time is what you need to give if you want to make a living with your writing.

If you're struggling to find the time, then how much do you really want this?

How much money is a 'living'?

When people think about making a living with their writing, they often assume it's about writing one incredible book and getting a traditional publishing deal with a huge advance, a movie deal and all the trappings of success. That is the dream and, in many cases, the myth of publishing. We hear stories of outliers getting seven-figure book deals and of course, there are tales of amazing success, but that's not the reality for most writers.

The top 1% of authors, the ones you know by name, are certainly making a lot of money, but most are not earning anywhere near that amount.

In 2018, the US Authors Guild reported that full-time traditionally published authors earned $12,400 on average. In May 2019, the UK Authors' Earnings and Contracts Report noted that the average annual earnings were £16,096 (approximately $20,000).

That's not what I call a living.

Self-published authors are no different. There are a few making multi-six and seven-figure incomes from their self-published books, a larger mid-list of writers who make at least five figures annually, and the vast majority who don't make money at all, and in fact may end up out of pocket.

But you don't have to be average.

You can take control of your author career, learn new skills, and apply them to your creative business.

Develop multiple streams of income

Back in 2008, I was working in a large IT department at a mining company in Brisbane, Australia. When the global financial crisis hit, they laid hundreds of us off in a single day and we all scrambled to find new work. At that point in my life, my job was my only source of income, and losing it so fast was shocking.

It was a wake-up call, and I decided never to rely on one company for all of my income again. I started developing multiple streams of income, which I continue to focus on as my primary business principle.

Nothing is stable, corporations least of all, and the global pandemic has only made that more clear as established business models disappeared overnight. The world is uncertain. You have to plan for change. Multiple streams of income can protect you because it's unlikely that they will all fail at the same time.

If you're reliant on a job or a single publisher, or you only use one self-publishing distributor, or you only have one client, one product, or one book, what risks might you face if the situation changes?

Making a living with your writing can be a long-term approach with money coming in every year for the rest of your creative life, and potentially up to 70 years after you die under copyright law. Multiple streams of income are the only way to ensure a resilient business for the long term.

Author, podcaster and speaker Sacha Black left her day job as a local government project manager two years ago. She says, "Multiple streams of income are the ultimate insurance policy for an author's business. While having different book formats is a good start, it doesn't guarantee a writer's financial security. If all our income comes from book sales, what happens if Amazon or any other distributor collapses or changes the rules? Jeff Bezos himself acknowledges that something will disrupt Amazon eventually.

Many authors get nervous when they hear 'multiple streams of income' because they think it will take time away from writing. It doesn't have to be like that. You have the power to design your income streams to suit your life and needs. Some of mine take up time, but others don't. That's how I like it. For example, you could invest in stocks or property, you could sell courses, or digital journals, do editing, create a Patreon platform, or even consult back into your old industry. The possibilities are endless."

You will also change the emphasis on different aspects of income over time as your creative journey continues.

Science fiction and fantasy author Ariele Sieling has income from self-publishing, Patreon, speaking, online courses, and merchandise.

She says, "The percentage each of these things has contributed to my overall income has changed significantly over the years. I've found it helpful to experiment with making money from a lot of different streams, but lately I've been shifting my focus toward the ones that are more reliable and fit in with my personality and process better, and leaning away from the ones that I either don't like doing or are less profitable (though I tend not to abandon anything completely in case I want to move back to it in the future)."

Do you believe you can make a living with your writing?

Your attitude to money is an important part of the mindset needed to be successful.

If you don't believe that you can make money with your writing, then that will be true for you. If you think authors who make six and seven-figure incomes are 'selling out,' then you're never going to make that amount, because it doesn't align with your values.

If you don't think you're good with money, then educate yourself. If you have a negative attitude toward wealth, then work on changing your mindset. Start with my recommended books at TheCreativePenn.com/moneybooks

Balance money for time with scalable income

In most jobs, you work for a certain number of hours and you are paid for your time. If you don't work, you don't get paid, or you are sacked at some point for not adhering to your contract. You're paid once for the hours that you work and you never get that time again. You have to keep exchanging time for money.

With scalable income, you spend your time once to create something of value, like a book, and then sell it over and over again. The time you spend upfront can bring in money month after month, year after year.

Let's say you spend a year of evenings and weekends writing your book, then editing and publishing it. That time is spent once, and that book might only sell a few copies. But it could sell a thousand, ten thousand, even a million copies. It could earn money for your lifetime plus 70 years after your death, if your estate is managed well.

This can feel like a risk if you're used to immediate money for time, but it is a fundamental mindset shift if you want to make a good living from your writing for the long term.

Most of us need a balance at the beginning, for example, keeping a day job or providing services like freelance writing or teaching to bring in immediate cash flow to pay the bills. But if you set aside a little time each week to build creative assets, you can change the balance over time.

In 2008, 100% of my income was time-based through my consulting day job. I was paid for the hours I worked and nothing more. Over the years, I have slowly created books and other assets and as I write this, over 80% of my income is scalable, earning money even if I'm not working.

How could you shift some of your income streams from time-based to scalable means?

Making a living from your writing is not just about writing

Many authors just want to write and have no interest in marketing or the business aspects of making money. They just want someone to handle all that for them.

But that's not the reality of being an author or making a living from your writing these days.

All authors have to market their books somehow, however they choose to publish. That might involve interviews and blog tours if you traditionally publish, or email marketing and paid ads if you go the indie route, but every author needs a platform these days.

Developing your writing craft and putting in the hours to create your books is only one half of making a living this way. You also need to embrace the other aspects if you want to increase your income.

I split my days into two. I create in the mornings, and I manage publishing, business and marketing tasks in the afternoon. Back when I had a day job, I would write between 5 am and 6 am, then go to work, and in the evenings, I'd spend an hour or so after dinner podcasting, connecting with authors, dealing with email and social media, reading books and taking courses to learn new skills.

These days, I'm a full-time creative, so I spend more time in each segment, but the principle remains the same. You need to set aside time to be creative, but also to learn new skills and market your work.

Embrace the growth mindset

Dr Carol Dweck coined the terms 'fixed and growth mindset' in her book, *Mindset: Changing the Way You Think to Fulfil Your Potential.*

The fixed mindset assumes that you are born with particular talents and intelligence, and you can't change that in any significant way. For example, writers are gifted and we can never achieve success because we weren't born with that kind of talent.

The growth mindset assumes that you can learn and develop new skills and that overcoming challenges will lead to progress. You can learn the art of writing and develop skills in marketing, business, and anything else you put your mind to.

If you want to make a living with your writing, you need to embrace the growth mindset. The world changes every day and we have to adapt. You can learn new writing skills, and you can also empower yourself with the knowledge you need to be successful.

I don't have a degree in creative writing, publishing, internet business or marketing, but I learned the skills I needed along the way. I found successful people to model and read their books, took courses, and attended conferences to learn everything I could. I put those lessons into practice for my own career, and I share what I learn with my audience along the way.

You can make a living with your writing. You just have to learn the skills and put them into action.

Urban fantasy author Angeline Trevena says, "Always be open to learning and trying new things, especially if it scares you. It's too easy to get stuck in a comfort rut, or to say that something doesn't work without really trying it. All of my biggest successes have been from pushing myself to do something that scared me!"

This book focuses on the practical side of making a living, but for more mindset tips, check out *The Successful Author Mindset*.

Model others who make a living from their writing

Back when I was in my miserable day job, I listened to podcast interviews on my commute to work every morning. I discovered Yaro Starak, an introvert, blogger and podcaster, who made enough money from his online business to buy a house and a car and invest. More importantly, he had the freedom to work when he liked, travel, and spend time with his family.

I knew I could achieve the same freedom because Yaro showed me it was possible. I downloaded his free Blog Profits Blueprint and did his course and started my website. I even wrote my own Author Blueprint to grow my email list by modeling his journey.

Yaro is still my mentor from afar, and I've interviewed him several times on my podcast over the years. But he is not an author, so I found others to model for that side of my writing business.

My author mentors include Kristine Kathryn Rusch, Dean Wesley Smith, and Orna Ross, writers with many decades of experience in the publishing industry and a deep knowledge of creativity and business skills.

None of these people have ever been 'official' mentors. I learn from their books, interviews, courses, and live events when available. That's the beauty of the writing life: We can learn from our mentors through their books!

It's important to find models who make money in the way that you want to, and whose career is still possible for you. For example, I am a huge Stephen King fan. I love his books and for a while, I thought he would be a good model for me. But although his writing influences my fiction, his career is not possible to emulate because he started back when publishing was a very different industry.

My personality is also different, and I am not content to focus my entire business on fiction. I am a multi-passionate creator, hence the multiple streams of income approach!

Find your different models based on the income streams you want to build, and these people may change over time as your focus shifts. Read blogs and books, listen to podcasts and audiobooks, attend events online or in person when possible, take courses, and listen to those whose voice and experience you trust — and who make money in the way you want to. If it's possible for them, it's possible for you.

Think long term

There are easier ways to make a living than with your writing and it's certainly not a get-rich-quick scheme. You want to create a body of work that you're proud of and that creates an income for the long term. It takes time to learn your craft and put the principles of creative business into practice.

But you're a writer. You love writing. So what else do you want to spend your life doing? Take it word by word, step by step, year by year, and you will achieve your goals.

Angie Scarr, non-fiction author and botanical miniaturist, says, "Writing is like investing in a pension plan. You have to be prepared for delayed gratification. Keep on stacking up those books."

Let's get into the details.

Questions:

- What is your definition of success?

- What will you do to achieve it?

- How much money is a 'living' for you? How much money do you want to make per year from your writing?

- Why are multiple streams of income important over the long term?

- Do you believe you can make a living with your writing? Do you need to work on your money mindset?

- How much of your income is money for time? How much is scalable? How could you shift this split?

- Writing is only one aspect of making a living with your writing. What are some other things you might need to learn?

- How will you embrace the growth mindset?

- Who are your models? How do they make money? Are those methods possible for you?

- If you don't have models in mind yet, how could you find them?

- Why is it important to think long term about making a living with your writing?

Resources:

- *The Successful Author Mindset: A Handbook for Surviving the Writer's Journey* — Joanna Penn

- *Mindset: Changing the Way You Think to Fulfil Your Potential* — Dr Carol Dweck

- *Your Author Business Plan: Take Your Author Career to the Next Level* — Joanna Penn

- List of useful money books and podcasts — www.TheCreativePenn.com/moneybooks

- Yaro Starak's Blog Profits Blueprint, regularly updated with best practices for making a living online — www.TheCreativePenn.com/BlogBlueprint

- Interview with Yaro Starak on freedom and long-term thinking — www.TheCreativePenn.com/yarofreedom

- Author Blueprint — www.TheCreativePenn.com/blueprint

- Authors Guild Report on author earnings — www.authorsguild.org/industry-advocacy/six-takeaways-from-the-authors-guild-2018-authors-income-survey/

- UK Authors' Earnings and Contracts 2018 — https://www.create.ac.uk/blog/2019/05/02/uk-authors-earnings-and-contracts-2018-a-survey-of-50000-writers/

- Books for writers by Kristine Kathryn Rusch and Dean Wesley Smith — www.wmgpublishinginc.com/writers

Part 1: How to Make Money with Books

1.1 Your publishing options and how the industry has changed

"The internet changed everything,
and more than two decades after it arrived,
it hasn't finished changing things yet."

Mike Shatzkin and Robert Paris Riger,
The Book Business: What Everyone Needs to Know

Publishing has changed as the internet shifted business models to global, digital solutions, and the opportunities for authors have expanded alongside this transformation. This in turn has encouraged creative empowerment and a growing confidence in the ability to connect directly with an audience, resulting in a digitally enabled renaissance for independent creators.

Wind the clock back 15 years and the only way to reach readers was through an agent and a publisher, advances were often enough to live on, and authors didn't have to do anything but write while someone else handled the marketing.

Perhaps that was only ever true for a select few, but it's certainly not the reality for authors in the 2020s. While there is a route to market through traditional publishing, opportunities for empowered creators continue to expand as technology enables us to reach readers in more countries with more formats of our books.

It is no longer a binary choice to traditionally publish or self-publish. Many successful authors choose to selectively license their rights — by book, by country or territory, by language, and by format.

In the following chapters, I'll outline your options around traditional publishing and self-publishing, also known as being an independent, or indie, author. But before we get into the details, it's important to look at how the publishing industry has shifted, and how those changes have accelerated due to the global pandemic.

A global, digital and mobile reading audience

Many writers focus on selling physical books in their local and national bookstores with marketing in country-specific mainstream media. While that is worth pursuing as one aspect of distribution, it ignores the huge and expanding global market of readers outside your home country and digital opportunities to reach them.

The biggest market for English language ebooks and audiobooks is still the US, UK, Canada and Australia, but over the last five years, my percentage of revenue has shifted more into other territories. You can reach readers in 190 countries with ebooks on mobile devices and tablets with the click of a button, and audiobooks are moving into an increasing number of territories through an expanding network of audio-first options.

The rise of the hyper-connected mobile economy means that global readers are discovering books through apps. You might not use them yourself or even have heard of them, but you can reach readers there through the ebook and audiobook distributors. Many readers don't live near a physical bookstore or want immediate consumption, so online retail drives entertainment, inspiration and education.

There's also a demographic trend toward streaming over ownership. Netflix, Amazon Prime, and Apple TV+ for TV and film; Spotify, Apple Music, or Tidal for music; Kindle Unlimited, Scribd, and Kobo Plus for ebooks; Audible, Storytel, and Scribd for audiobooks; with more subscription options emerging every year.

Of course, readers still love print books and buy a lot of them, but increasingly they purchase print online. Publishing Perspectives noted in August 2020 that, "In print books, Amazon has a generally recognized 50 percent or more of the American market."

You can reach readers who purchase print online through Amazon KDP Print, and use Ingram Spark to reach physical bookstore catalogs, libraries, universities, and other print-on-demand services globally, as well as Bookshop. org, which supports independent booksellers with online sales in the US and UK.

If you want to make a living from your writing, then expand your horizons, because most of your income is likely to come from the rest of the world, not your local bookstore. There's more detail on how you can reach readers globally in section 1.8.

Digital reading and online book purchasing have accelerated because of the pandemic

The global, digital, mobile business model proved its resilience when the pandemic hit. Many people found solace in reading as the world shut down and many indie authors, myself included, sold more books and reached more readers than ever before.

A McKinsey report in October 2020 noted that, "responses to COVID-19 have speeded up the adoption of digital technologies by several years — and many of these changes could be here for the long haul … Consumers have moved dramatically toward online channels and companies and industries have responded in turn."

When physical bookstores shut down, readers bought print online or tried ebooks and audiobooks for the first time. Libraries accelerated the adoption of ebook and audiobook lending. Even readers in countries traditionally resistant to digital, like France and Italy, experienced growth in these areas, and book marketing moved online.

While there will certainly be a return to buying in physical stores once the pandemic is over, people's behavior has shifted and it's likely that digital adoption is here to stay.

The Maker Movement

"Makers are producers and creators, builders and shapers of the world around us. Makers are people who regard technology as an invitation to explore and experiment… If you want to make, there has never been a better time."

Dale Dougherty, *Free to Make: How the Maker Movement is Changing our Schools, Our Jobs and Our Minds*

The Maker Movement represents a shift from faceless corporations churning out widgets in factories to the artisan creator producing individual work and selling it directly to consumers who want to support independent artists.

It encompasses physical maker spaces where people use 3D printing to prototype ideas, as well as those using open source code to create new programs and games, independent musicians, filmmakers and writers who use the internet to distribute, and those who make art to sell on Etsy or at local markets, plus so many more.

It represents a shift from passive consumption to a renaissance of creativity at all stages of life, empowering individuals to make and explore, to play and try new things, and for some, to change the way they make a living.

Consumers love to support independent creators because their work is more original and authentic and they know that their money goes to support the individual's art, as opposed to propping up mega-corporations.

Consider your own purchasing behavior. Do you listen to independent musicians or watch independent films? Do you enjoy drinking locally brewed small-batch beer, or buy artisan bread directly from a local baker instead of the supermarket? Do you buy vegetables at your local farmers' market? Do you buy art and craft gift items from Etsy? Have you supported a creative project on Kickstarter or Patreon? Have you bought a book directly from an author?

The empowerment of the creator

These technological and cultural shifts put the power back into the hands of those creatives who choose to take hold of their careers.

You can write and publish what you want, when you want, and reach readers however you choose. Your career is in your hands. You can work with publishers to get your books into the world, you can work with freelancers and do it yourself, or you can choose a combination of both.

Award-winning and international bestselling author, J.D. Barker, spent over twenty years as a ghostwriter before producing suspense thrillers under his own name. After initial success as an indie author with *Forsaken*, J.D. attracted traditional publishing deals, as well as film and TV options, and he now chooses his route to market per book, territory, format, and language. He shares his thoughts on publishing on the Writers, Ink Podcast, co-hosted with J. Thorn. J.D. is one of the most successful hybrid authors I know, so I asked him for his thoughts on how things have changed in the publishing industry.

"I remember when Stephen King published *Riding the Bullet* back in March of 2000, certainly the first ebook by a mainstream author. For a whopping $2.50 I downloaded all 33 pages and devoured it as I had everything else he'd written. He crashed the Simon & Schuster website with what seemed like a stunt.

Who knew. eBooks. eReaders. KDP, Nook, Kobo … the publishing world had been the same for a thousand years, then one day it wasn't.

As you're reading this, some pimple-faced sixteen-year-old kid is busy creating whatever will come next. While many in the publishing world see this as frightening, others see it as opportunity. I like to think the years I have in this industry put me in that latter group.

When I first started back in 1990, the talk was how readership was declining, book stores were going out of business, publishing deals hard to come by … yada, yada, yada. The truth is, as long as people want to hear a story they'll need someone to tell it. How you get it to them is entirely up to you.

As authors, today's publishing world offers more choices than ever before. You can go the query/agent/publisher 'traditional' route or (if you're willing to do the work) you can get your words out there all on your own. To the end reader, the path you choose doesn't really matter. Most will never know. As long as your story is a good story, that is.

Indie publishing should never be your 'Plan B.' I've lost count of the number of people who have told me, "Well, if I can't get a trad deal, I'll just publish it myself."

No. No. No.

That's not what this is about.

If your writing isn't good enough to get you a traditional deal, you need to hit the pause button and figure out why.

The authors who are successful in the indie world, the ones making a career out of it, could get traditional deals but choose not to.

In my case, I consider all options for each book and I go with whatever makes the most business sense for a particular title. I mix things up and take the 'hybrid' approach. Some of my titles are with traditional publishers, others are indie published through my own small press. Sometimes, I take it even further — I have several books that are indie published in some territories and traditionally published in others. Hybrid books within a hybrid model.

What's going to earn me the most? What will get the book in front of the largest audience? What will raise my profile (and help me sell more books)?

Don't be afraid to ask questions.

Don't be afraid to say no.

Don't be afraid to walk away.

Nothing is carved in stone. Keep it fluid.

To succeed in today's publishing world, you need to be nimble. You need to adapt.

We've never had more options than we do today, and that's a beautiful thing."

Questions:

- What are the opportunities for your book/s if you consider the market to be global, digital, and mobile?

- What are some shifts to digital business that you've seen or read about due to the pandemic?

- How has your own reading and purchasing behavior changed over the last decade?

- How do you currently support independent creators in the way you choose to purchase?

- How could you embrace the Maker Movement as part of your own creative journey?

- Do you consider yourself an empowered creator? How could you move further toward this in order to expand your creative potential?

Resources:

- *Free To Make: How the Maker Movement is Changing our Schools, Our Jobs and Our Minds* — Dale Dougherty

- *Makers: The New Industrial Revolution* — Chris Anderson

- Writers, Ink Podcast with hybrid author J.D. Barker and indie authors J. Thorn and Zach Bohannon. Conversations with traditional and indie authors around the publishing industry — WritersInkPodcast.com

- *The Book Business: What Everyone Needs to Know* — Mike Shatzkin and Robert Paris Riger

1.2 Your book is a valuable intellectual property asset

"Writers do *not* sell books. We license copyright."

Kristine Kathryn Rusch,
Rethinking the Writing Business

Many authors think that when they finish a manuscript, they have just one book to show for it.

But it is much more than that.

Once the penny drops on how rights licensing works, you will truly see the value in your writing.

This is just an overview, so please read the suggested books and resources quoted to empower yourself further in this important area.

What is copyright?

"Copyright is a legal device that provides the creator of a work of art or literature, or a work that conveys information or ideas, the right to control how the work is used."

Stephen Fishman, *The Copyright Handbook:*
What Every Writer Needs To Know

Copyright is a form of intellectual property, similar to patents, trademarks and design assets. Like physical property, it can be licensed or transferred, and it is the basis of the contracts you will sign, however you choose to publish. It can be defined as an asset as it has value and is created with the expectation of future reward and can be included on a company balance sheet.

You have copyright in your work once it exists in tangible form. It's not necessary to register your manuscript, but it may provide more protection in any legal disputes if you do.

As the copyright holder, you control how the work is used. You license the right to reproduce the book, to distribute and sell it, to create adaptations and derivative works (for example, screenplays or translations), and/or to perform or display the work in public.

You don't have to license everything all at once to the same company, and in fact, you usually don't want to. The best way to make money with your copyright is to carve it up into different slices and make the most of every piece.

As Dean Wesley Smith says in *The Magic Bakery*, "Say you write a novel. The novel is the pie. The copyright is what you license from the pie, the pieces of the pie … You never sell the entire pie."

You can slice your copyright pie up in different ways.

One slice might be Paperback rights for UK Commonwealth in English which you license to a traditional publisher. Another slice might be Worldwide English ebook rights which you decide to license non-exclusively to specific distributors like Amazon for Kindle, Kobo, Apple, and Google Play, as well as selling direct to readers from your website. Yet another slice might be South Korean language and territory rights to ebook, paperback and hardback editions for a limited term of seven years.

All for the same book, with many more slides of the pie remaining.

In broad terms, think about format, language, territory (or country), and time frame. You can slice the pie up in as many ways as you can imagine.

It's magic because you receive money for a slice, and then it can return to you later in order to license all over again. For example, I licensed German ebook rights to one of my novels several years ago, and the rights returned to me after three years so I could continue selling it myself, or re-license it if preferred. This is even more magical for short stories, which you can license for reprint and anthologies multiple times after the first serial rights.

You can find more detail on different rights licensing in *The Copyright Handbook* by Stephen Fishman.

Why is it important to understand rights licensing?

Publishers are not charities.

They license copyright and publish books in order to make money. Of course, most people working within the publishing industry truly love books and literary culture, but a business needs to make a profit over the long-term.

Consider a publishing contract clause that is all too common these days which licenses, "All languages, all territories, all formats now existing and to be invented, for the term of copyright."

The term of copyright is 50 or 70 years after the death of the author depending on your jurisdiction, so this clause really is the whole pie!

If you consider the possibilities of selective rights licensing, do you really want to sign such an all-encompassing contract term?

Is any single company going to be able to make the most of every slice of your magic pie, even for formats that have not been invented yet? Or is it better to license selectively based on the company's specialization?

As Stephen Fishman says in *The Copyright Handbook*, "It is usually in an author's best interest to retain as many rights as possible, unless, of course, the publisher pays so much that it makes sense to assign all rights."

You will have to define what 'so much' means to you, but many authors undervalue their work and license everything for just a few thousand dollars because they don't truly understand what they are signing.

Many authors take deals because they're grateful they have been offered anything at all, but you need to value your writing if you want to make a living from it. Remember, contracts are for negotiating.

Won't my agent handle all this?

If you work with a good agent, they will help you with your contracts as part of their job in exchange for 15% commission, but this is your copyright, your career, and your money on the line. If you empower yourself with knowledge around contract terms and licensing, you will save yourself heartache, time and money along the way, especially if you are considering writing as a career.

However you choose to publish, author organizations like The Authors Guild and the Society of Authors, as well as the Alliance of Independent Authors, can help with understanding contract terms.

Selective rights licensing or the hybrid model

"Some people call authors who both self-publish and trade-publish 'hybrid.' At the Alliance of Independent Authors, it's just part of being indie... The indie author licenses rights selectively, with a sense of their own worth and their books' value. For us, trade publishers are author services, not the other way around, and rights deals are all just part of being indie."

Orna A. Ross, *Creative Self-Publishing: Make and Sell Your Books Your Way*

The most successful authors understand the importance of selective rights licensing, and work with a combination of companies to maximize their returns. It is no longer either traditional publishing or self-publishing; it is a combination of both.

J.K. Rowling retained her digital rights to Harry Potter and started her company, Pottermore, in 2008 to distribute ebooks and audiobooks, moving into other partnerships and business ventures over time. According to the Financial Times in June 2017, it is now a $25 billion business.

Of course, most of us will never reach that level of success, but many authors selectively license to make more money and reach more readers, many of whom are quoted throughout this book.

Mark Dawson, bestselling author of the John Milton thriller series, self-publishes his ebooks in English exclusively with Amazon, as well as licensing English language print editions to Welbeck Publishing Group and audio projects to Audible among others.

Children's author Karen Inglis licensed *The Secret Lake* to publishers in Russia, Turkey, Albania, the Czech Republic, China, Iran, and Ukraine. All approached her after the book's self-published success on Amazon in English.

Fantasy author Brandon Sanderson licenses his books to traditional publishers, but retains the right to special editions. In November 2020, Sanderson raised nearly US$7 million on Kickstarter to create the 10th anniversary leather-bound special edition of *The Way of Kings*.

Authors with decades of experience in the publishing industry combine different rights licensing deals for their books into a highly lucrative career. I recommend books by Kristine Kathryn Rusch, Dean Wesley Smith, and Orna Ross on this topic as they have extensive experience in every side of the industry.

Hopefully, you now understand the value of your copyright and how licensing it in various ways can bring you multiple streams of income. Let's get into the detail of your publishing options.

Questions:

- What is copyright?

- How does rights licensing make you money?

- Why is selective rights licensing a good idea?

- How can you empower yourself with the knowledge you need in this area?

Resources:

- *The Copyright Handbook: What Every Writer Needs To Know* — Stephen Fishman

- *Rethinking The Writing Business* — Kristine Kathryn Rusch

- *Selective Rights Licensing: Sell Your Book Rights At Home and Abroad* — Orna A. Ross and Helen Sedwick

- *Creative Self-Publishing: Make and Sell Your Books Your Way* — Orna A. Ross

- *The Magic Bakery: Copyright in the Modern World of Fiction Publishing* — Dean Wesley Smith

- *Closing the Deal ... on Your Terms: Agents, Contracts and Other Considerations* — Kristine Kathryn Rusch

- *Hollywood vs. The Author* — Edited by Stephen Jay Schwartz

- Empowering authors around copyright. Interview with Rebecca Giblin — TheCreativePenn.com/rebeccagiblin

- The importance of editing and why authors need to understand their publishing contracts with Ruth Ware — www.TheCreativePenn.com/ruthware

- The Society of Authors (UK) — SocietyOfAuthors.org

- The Authors Guild (USA) — AuthorsGuild.org

- The Alliance of Independent Authors (global) — AllianceIndependentAuthors.org

1.3 Traditional publishing

> "Play whatever game you want to play. Just make sure
> you're clear about why you're playing it."

Mark McGuinness, *21 Insights for 21st Century Creatives*

Traditional or trade publishing refers to the long-established system of getting a book deal through submission to agents, who will submit the manuscript to publishers with the hope of a book deal that eventually leads to publication.

There are many benefits to traditional publishing.

Prestige, kudos, and validation

For many authors, the goal of publication is critical acclaim, acceptance within the industry, and validation that their work is 'good enough.' There is a hierarchy of publishing houses and imprints, and certain literary prizes only accept traditionally published books.

Non-fiction authors may also want to pursue this route, as a traditional deal may open up new business opportunities, such as speaking events, that they might not be able to access through other routes.

If your definition of success includes a traditional deal because of these reasons, then nothing else will do. Embrace your need for validation and start pitching agents — but you'll need a different book for that!

An established, professional team to manage the editorial and publication process

Your agent may have editorial comments on your manuscript before it's submitted. If you get a book deal, you'll work with an editor and proofreader at the publishing company and you may have input into the book cover design process.

Some authors specifically target agents and publishers based on editorial excellence, but you can't always guarantee getting the editor of your choice.

Significant marketing help

Many authors just want to write and have no interest in marketing their work, but increasingly, authors have to do their own marketing or at least play a part in the publisher's activities around book launch.

The level of marketing activity is usually determined by the publisher's investment in the book, with more significant deals getting the most support.

There are some publishers who excel at marketing. Dean Koontz signed a five-book deal with Amazon Publishing's Thomas and Mercer imprint in July 2019, saying in Publishers Weekly that Amazon "presented a marketing and publicity plan smarter and more ambitious than anything I'd ever seen before … The times are changing, and it's invigorating to be where change is understood and embraced."

Upfront payment (advance) and no financial cost to publish

Authors are usually paid an advance against royalties as part of a traditional publishing deal, although there are an increasing number of alternative models where authors take little or no upfront advance with higher royalty payments later. The amount will vary based on how much the publisher expects to make from the book, the sales history of the author, their platform, and many other factors.

In June 2020, 2800 authors anonymously shared their publishing deals on Twitter as part of #publishingpaidme which highlighted the disparities of payments to authors of color, as well as differences between genres, gender, and debut vs. established authors. The advances range from several hundred to several million dollars with everything in between. You can find the spreadsheet at:

TheCreativePenn.com/publishingpaidme

The advance is against royalties, which are usually 7-25% of the net book price. If you get an advance of $10,000, the book has to earn more than $10,000 in royalties before you receive any more money. When authors talk of a book 'earning out,' it has made back the advance and is now in profit, so the author will start receiving additional royalty payments.

There are no upfront costs in a traditional publishing deal. If you're asked for money by a publisher, then it is an author services company or hybrid publisher where the costs and quality vary significantly. You can find more detail in the next chapter on self-publishing.

Print distribution to bookstores

Traditional publishing excels at print distribution with physical bookstores as their main channel for sales. Sales reps manage store relationships and make it easy for book buyers to select books and pay later minus any returns. Books are usually in store for a month or two and only remain if they are perennial sellers.

The global pandemic severely disrupted this model as physical bookstores closed and print purchases moved online where print-on-demand books have an advantage as they never go out of stock. Publishers Weekly reported 2020 as a record year for ebook and print sales, with backlist titles, which are easier to find online, accounting for 67% of print purchases.

Higher chance of subsidiary rights licensing

Many literary agencies also focus on licensing for subsidiary rights, including foreign territories, and film and TV. Authors can receive additional income from these licenses which range significantly in terms of deal income and timeline.

While some bestselling indie authors have attracted these kinds of deals, it's certainly not as common.

A chance to play the 'literary lottery'

There are only a few household name authors in the world — Stephen King, Dan Brown, J. K. Rowling, James Patterson, and Nora Roberts are a few examples. These are the superstar writers, most of whom have been writing for many years and have built their careers over decades.

Then there are the breakout authors and books whose names we know because of the significance of their deals, like Paula Hawkins for *The Girl on the Train*, or those turned into successful film or TV, like Julia Quinn's *Bridgerton* series.

Of course, we would all love this kind of breakout success, but you can't build a sustainable living on the possibility of a winning lottery ticket or lightning strike. Yes, there is a chance that your book will be the next big thing, but the odds are most definitely against you, especially in an increasingly fragmented media world.

* * *

So what are the downsides to the traditional route?

Slow process

Writing and editing your book will take the same amount of time regardless of how you choose to publish, but it may take months or even years to get an agent if you're just starting out, then more time to get a publishing deal, and then still more time for the book to reach publication. For many authors, it may be several years between finishing a manuscript and seeing it on the shelves, although publishers can also get a book out quickly if it is time critical.

Loss of creative control

While your book will always be your book, many authors do not have control over aspects of packaging such as the title, description, and positioning in a genre.

If you are successful with a book, the publisher will probably want more in the same vein, so an author can feel trapped within one particular genre. Many authors change their names when switching genres or if their sales slump over time and they need to start again.

Novelist and poet Orna Ross describes the clash of expectations over her historical Irish novel, *After The Rising*. "Where I saw a page-turning drama that shattered silences and explored themes of freedom and belonging, my publisher saw what was then called 'chick lit.'"

The book went to the top of the charts, but Orna describes it as a "bruising experience," and as a result of short-sighted marketing, her next book launch didn't go so well. She later found creative freedom through self-publishing and founded the Alliance of Independent Authors to help others on the same path.

Lower royalty rates and lack of transparency in reporting

Royalty rates are usually a percentage of the net sale of the book, not the cover price. All the discounts, returns, marketing costs, and overheads are taken off the total before your percentage is calculated.

Royalty rates for traditional publishing usually range between 7% and 25%, although some may be higher if there is a smaller advance, and all vary by contract terms.

Reports on sales and royalties usually arrive every six months, and many authors report how difficult they are to understand and reconcile with payments. As more publishers move into digital sales, some are developing author portals with more up-to-date information, similar to the dashboards that independent authors can access with almost real-time sales and revenue.

Lack of significant marketing help

I included marketing in the positive side of traditional publishing above because some publishers do an incredible job.

On the flip side, you will often hear complaints from authors that their publisher does not do enough marketing for them, especially after the initial launch. It will depend on the book and the publisher, so be sure to ask for a marketing plan as part of contract negotiations.

Beware of potentially prohibitive contract clauses

You license your copyright by signing a contract and even if you have an agent to help you, it is still your responsibility to understand the terms and only sign what you consider to be the right deal for you.

Even before you reach the publishing stage, you might sign an agency agreement, which also differ in their terms. I was once offered a contract that included a clause where the agency would receive 15% of *everything* I published, regardless of whether or not they sold the work, including my self-published work.

I didn't sign that contract.

In terms of your publishing contract, it is generally better to limit the terms as much as possible, as discussed in the previous chapter.

Contracts are for negotiation, so discuss the following with your agent and/or publisher:

- What countries or territories will the book be published in? If it won't be available everywhere, then why license World English?

- What formats are specified? For example, if audiobook rights are included, how long will it be before the audiobook is published and in which territories?

- What subsidiary rights are included, and how will these be exploited? Many publishers will sub-license foreign languages or may license for film/TV and other media.

- How long is the contract for? Is it term-limited, for example, five years for foreign language rights? When and how will the rights revert? For example, if the audiobook is not produced within three years, the rights revert to the author.

- Is there a 'do not compete' clause which may prevent you publishing during the term of the contract under the same name, in the same world or with the same characters?

You do not need to be a lawyer to understand contract terms, although some authors do engage legal professionals to help. Many author organizations like The Authors Guild (US) and the Society of Authors (UK), as well as the Alliance of Independent Authors, have resources and help for understanding contract clauses and negotiation.

I also recommend *Closing the Deal ... on Your Terms: Agents, Contracts and Other Considerations* by Kristine Kathryn Rusch.

The money side of traditional publishing

This book is about making a living, so it's important to consider how the money works for traditional publishing.

In May 2019, the UK Authors' Earnings and Contracts Report noted that the average earnings were £16,096 (approximately $20,000). Only 69% of authors received an advance, with publishers citing the need to split the risk of publication with the author.

They also describe a 'winner takes all' situation where the top 10% of writers earn around 70% of total earnings. The publishing press, especially around book fair time, focus on the big six- and seven-figure deals, skewing the perception of author income, whereas most writers receive nowhere near this.

The Financial Times reported in June 2019 that, "A senior independent literary publisher in the UK told me she offers advances of £3000-£5000, only occasionally going up to £10,000."

This payment is usually split, with a percentage on signing, a further amount on acceptance of the manuscript, and a final payment on publication, plus royalties later if the book earns out.

Some authors make additional revenue from subsidiary rights licensing, with foreign rights, TV and film adaptations, and audiobook deals. But the reality is that most traditionally published authors need multiple streams of income just as much as anyone else. Most have a day job, or teach writing, or work as editors, as covered in Part 2.

Would I take a traditional publishing deal?

Absolutely.

In fact, I have several publishing deals for books in foreign languages and different territories, and I am always open to licensing my intellectual property assets — if the conditions and contract terms are right for a project.

You must make your own decision on how to publish, but make sure that you empower yourself with the knowledge you need to understand your contract and the impact any choice will have on your author career.

Questions:

- What are the benefits of traditional publishing?

- What are the downsides of traditional publishing?

- How does the money work?

- Are you considering this route to publication? What are your reasons for this? What is your definition of success?

- How could you take the next step?

Resources:

- *Closing the Deal … on Your Terms: Agents, Contracts and Other Considerations* — Kristine Katherine Rusch

- *Selective Rights Licensing: Sell Your Book Rights At Home and Abroad* — Orna A. Ross and Helen Sedwick

- *Creative Self-Publishing: Make and Sell Your Books Your Way* — Orna A. Ross and the Alliance of Independent Authors

- *The Book Business: What Everyone Needs to Know* — Mike Shatzkin and Robert Paris Riger

- *Writers' and Artists' Yearbook* — Published annually by Bloomsbury in the UK. Listing of agents, publishers, awards and much more within the traditional publishing industry. They also have an online portal www.writersandartists.co.uk

- #PublishingPaidMe list of advances — TheCreativePenn.com/publishingpaidme

- Writers, Ink Podcast with hybrid author J.D. Barker and indie authors J. Thorn and Zach Bohannon. Conversations with traditional and indie authors around the publishing industry — WritersInkPodcast.com

- How publishing has changed, the importance of reading your contracts, changing pen names and more with psychological thriller author, Ruth Ware — TheCreativePenn.com/ruthware

- How to find and pitch a literary agent. Interview with Barbara Poelle — TheCreativePenn.com/barbarapoelle

- The Authors Guild (US) — AuthorsGuild.org

- The Society of Authors (UK) — SocietyOfAuthors.org

- Alliance of Independent Authors — TheCreativePenn.com/alliance

- CREATe UK Authors' Earnings and Contracts 2018: A Survey of 50,000 Writers — Create.ac.uk/uk-authors-earnings-and-contracts-2018-a-survey-of-50000-writers

1.4 Self-publishing or becoming an indie author

"The only obstacle today to becoming an author is yourself. Stop making excuses."

Alastair Humphreys, Author and Adventurer

It is now possible to reach readers all over the world with your books in multiple formats through online services. In fact, once you get the hang of it, publishing is the easy part. Writing and marketing remain the key challenge for authors, however you choose to publish.

This section provides an overview of options if you choose to manage publishing yourself. For more details, check out *Successful Self-Publishing: How to Self-Publish and Market Your Book*, available as a free ebook and also in print and audio editions.

Self-publishing is nothing new

Walt Whitman self-published *Leaves of Grass*, Jane Austen paid Thomas Egerton to publish *Sense and Sensibility*, Beatrix Potter self-published *The Tale of Peter Rabbi*t, and William Blake wrote the text, drew the illustrations, and self-published *Songs of Innocence and of Experience*, among many other notable literary examples.

Authors have also started small presses to publish their own work and books by author friends. Virginia Woolf and her husband, Leonard, started Hogarth Press in 1917, "a business that could potentially free the couple from the whims of publishers and even a social outlet through which their diverse literary friendships could be monetised," according to The Guardian.

What's the difference between self-publishing and being an indie (or independent) author?

The term self-publishing implies doing everything yourself. There's certainly nothing wrong with that, and it's wonderful to create books in the world for the sheer love of creation. I helped my nine-year-old niece to self-publish her first book, and I helped my dad to self-publish *Nada*, a historical thriller, for his 65th birthday. These were one-off creative projects with no commercial intent.

But this book is about making a living with your writing, so the term independent author, or indie author, is more appropriate and it's certainly the term I prefer. I work with professional freelance editors and cover designers to create quality products, and invest in marketing to reach readers. As much as writing is my art, it's also my business, not a hobby.

Of course, many authors start out self-publishing and transition over time as they gain experience and knowledge. We all start at the beginning and learn along the way.

* * *

There are many benefits to being an indie author.

Creative control over content and design

You are free to write and publish what you choose — but of course, that freedom comes with a learning curve! There will always be genres that sell better than others, so the principles of book marketing always apply.

You have creative control over the look and feel of your book. There are free and cheap options for cover design, and easy-to-use formatting software. However, I definitely recommend working with a professional book cover designer to package your book effectively.

You can also change your books over time. You can re-edit, easily create a new edition, change your cover design and even your book titles, all of which I have done over the last decade. Just upload a new set of files.

Speed to market

This is the reason I went indie in the first place. I considered the timeline of traditional publishing for my first book, how it would take months or years to get an agent, and then months or years to get a contract, and then more time before the book hit the shelves. I didn't want to wait that long.

Of course, you still have to spend the same amount of time writing and editing, but once you're ready to publish, you can upload your files to the various services and your ebook and print book can be on sale within 24 hours. Audiobooks take longer on the major platforms, but you can sell them immediately from your author website. You can receive income from the book 60 days later, or even the same day with direct sales.

Publish globally in all formats

If you own and control your intellectual property rights, you can publish and sell your books in 190 countries, many of those in print and audio as well as ebook formats. When you upload your book to the various platforms, just select the option for world rights. No need to ask permission from anyone.

Many traditionally published authors license World English rights for all formats and yet have barely sold outside their specific country markets because their books aren't available there. Many have also licensed audiobook rights, but the books have not been produced in audio.

As discussed in section 1.2, you can have the best of both worlds through selective rights licensing. If you're traditionally published in some markets, revisit your contract. Consider self-publishing in countries where you haven't yet licensed the rights, or in formats you still control. You might be leaving money on the table otherwise.

Sell niche books or market to specific audiences

Publishing companies need a certain number of sales for a book to be worthwhile, so they may not choose to publish a book if the audience is too small, especially if you consider territory- or country-specific markets. But niche readership may well be enough to satisfy your definition of success and bring in additional revenue, even more so if you publish globally, which expands the market.

If you already have a niche audience, it can be more lucrative to self-publish. For example, bloggers and podcasters, as well as business owners, often self-publish and sell direct in order to maximize their creative choices and revenue streams.

Higher royalties

Most ebook retailers offer royalties of 30-70%, and if you sell direct, you can take over 90% royalty, covered in more detail in section 1.9. Traditional royalty rates usually range from 7% to 25%, with some as high as 50%, varying by specific contract terms, so you need to sell far fewer books to make the same amount of money with self-publishing.

For print-on-demand books, you can set your own profit margin. I usually make around US$2 per book. Audiobook royalties vary by platform, usually 25-50%, again with 90% if you sell direct.

For a comparison of royalties between the traditional and indie models, check out #1 New York Times and USA Today bestselling author Ilona Andrews' blog at:

www.ilona-andrews.com/2021/flowers-and-questions

But of course, self-publishing is not a get-rich-quick scheme. You can't guarantee that you're going to make as many sales as you would have done with a traditional publisher, or indeed, any sales at all. You cannot just upload your book and expect it to make you money. Section 1.10 goes into aspects of marketing.

Empowerment

The American Psychological Association reported that "freedom and personal autonomy are more important to people's well-being than money," and indie authors certainly have these!

It might take months or even years of rejection and criticism to get an agent and even after signing a contract, traditionally published authors have very little control — over pricing, timing of publication, marketing, sometimes over the cover, the title, and even the words themselves. Plenty of authors are told to change their books to fit what an agent or publisher wants.

Compare that to the empowerment of the indie author. Write and publish what you want, as fast as you like. Learn new skills, work with professionals, make mistakes and learn from them, earn money directly, and interact with your readers.

Yes, it's hard work, but it's certainly empowering if you take control!

Stop asking permission. You don't need it.

Stop waiting to be chosen. Choose yourself.

Attract a traditional publishing deal

Many indie authors choose to work with traditional publishers, and if you're successful, agents and publishers will come to you. The power balance is reversed and the empowered indie can often get a much better deal than a first-time author with no evidence of sales or marketing platform.

Hugh Howey took a print-only deal after his success with *Wool*, Andy Weir attracted a movie deal for *The Martian* after originally self-publishing the ebook on Amazon, and E. L. James made multi-millions from *Fifty Shades of Grey* after originally self-publishing the books.

While those are some big names, there are many indie authors who license foreign rights, or different formats, to publishers based on their independent success.

Of course, it's not all roses and kittens as an indie author! There are downsides.

No prestige, kudos or validation by the established industry

Attitudes have shifted over the last decade, but there are still some who consider self-published books to be second rate. They see the choice to go indie as 'vanity' instead of a savvy business decision by an empowered creative entrepreneur.

Most literary prizes don't accept indie books and most literary critics for mainstream media won't review them, although the Alliance of Independent Authors is trying to change this with the Open Up To Indie Authors campaign.

If your definition of success is based on what traditionally published authors, agents, and publishers think of you, then indie might not be the best route for you.

You need to up-skill or find and manage freelancers

As with any new direction, going indie can be a steep learning curve. You need to write and market your book, but you also have to do the publishing. You have to find an editor and a cover designer, decide on the title and sales description, format your manuscript for different versions, and find suitable professionals to help.

This may sound daunting, but it's easier than it used to be, as the indie author community share recommendations, tips and best practices online. You can also join the Alliance of Independent Authors, which vets service providers to make sure you get a good deal.

You will need to manage these tasks yourself, or find someone to help you. It is definitely a challenge at the beginning, but once you have your team in place, you just repeat the process with each book and it gets easier every time.

I love (almost) all aspects of being an indie author. It suits my personality and the way I like to work. If you can manage a small project or you want to learn the appropriate skills, then you'll likely enjoy it too.

"Being an indie author is a wonderful job, with a high level of creative and commercial freedom, but that's not to say that self-publishing is easy. To be an author, to be a publisher, to run a creative business: these are three challenging ambitions, all rolled into one indie author. You."

Orna A. Ross, *Creative Self-Publishing:*
Make and Sell Your Books Your Way

You need a budget upfront if you want a professional result

These days, you're likely to invest in professional editing before submitting to an agent anyway, or at least buy books and courses for writers. Everyone spends on their hobby, so whether you're knitting or writing or mountain biking, most people are happy to allocate money they never get back on something they love.

However, if you want to make a living this way, then you need to invest money in creating assets for your business with the intention of getting it back through multiple streams of income. Either way, you need a budget upfront if you want to be a professional indie author.

Between 2006-2011, I funded my new writing career from my day job. As I made money, I reinvested it in the business until I had enough assets and income streams to take a salary and dividends. I go into this in more detail in *Your Author Business Plan: Take Your Author Career to the Next Level.*

It's difficult to get print distribution in bookstores

"Economies of scale mean that few of us can compete with trade publishing in the print-book-to-bookstore model," says Orna Ross in *Creative Self-Publishing*. "The economics of physical bookstore distribution—given the discounts retailers, wholesalers, and distributors need to make their profits—are punishing, even for big publishers."

While many indie authors are frustrated by this, an increasing number of readers buy print books online, behavior that accelerated as the pandemic shut down physical stores, so print-on-demand options will make your books available to many readers.

However, it is possible to get your indie books into bookstores. If you publish through Ingram Spark, your books are listed in the catalogs that bookstores, libraries, and universities use and also available through online print-on-demand sites worldwide. You can specify significant discounts and even allow returns, as well as managing bulk orders on behalf of retailers. You can use a site like Bookshop.org to benefit independent booksellers with online sales.

Although I choose to focus on digital sales first, my books have been stocked in physical stores in the US and UK, as well as at university campus bookstores, libraries, and literary festivals — all because I publish print editions through Ingram Spark as well as KDP Print.

For more detail, check out *An Author's Guide to Working with Libraries and Bookstores* by Mark Leslie Lefebvre, and *Winning Shelf Space: How to Get Your Self-Published Book into Bookstores* by Debbie Young and Orna A. Ross

How to self-publish your book

Once you have written and edited your book, you'll need book cover design and formatting to prepare it for publication.

There are various distributors you can use depending on the format, and while some have minor charges, most are free to publish while taking a cut of sales. They only make money when you make money.

Personally, I publish direct through Amazon KDP, Kobo Writing Life, and Apple Books for ebooks, as well as using distributors Draft2Digital and PublishDrive to reach Google Play, Nook, Tolino and many more, as well as library services.

I use Amazon KDP Print and Ingram Spark for paperback, large print, and hardback editions, and I use ACX and Findaway Voices for audiobooks.

While this might sound a lot, most of the interfaces are similar and require the same files and metadata like book description, price, etc. Once you have done it a couple of times, it only takes a few hours to publish a book.

Exclusivity vs. wide publishing

There are some specific retailer programs that require exclusivity. The most significant are Amazon KDP Select, which includes your ebooks in Kindle Unlimited (KU), and ACX for audiobooks. If you opt into these exclusive contracts, you cannot publish on other platforms and you are limited to a particular audience in specific territories. In return, you get higher royalties, different marketing options, and in some cases, better visibility.

Importantly, you can still publish on these platforms and choose the non-exclusive publishing option.

Some authors do incredibly well publishing exclusively, and others find it doesn't work at all. You can choose per book and there are time-limited terms, so you can change your mind later and opt in or out as you choose.

It's important to do your own research and decide what's best for you and your books. Two Facebook communities represent different ends of the spectrum: 20BooksTo50K focuses primarily on success within KU, and WideForTheWin offers advice and support for authors choosing the wide (non-exclusive) model.

You are empowered to make your own choice. No one can choose for you. That's the power — and the pain — of being an indie author!

Other publishing options

So far, I've covered the two extreme ends of the publishing spectrum — traditional and self-publishing — but these days, there are many more options for authors, including the hybrid model outlined in section 1.1.

Author and publishing industry expert Jane Friedman has a downloadable chart which gives a wider view of the spectrum of possibilities at TheCreativePenn.com/publishingpaths

You, the creator, are empowered to choose per book how you would like to take it to market. Just make sure you understand the ramifications before you sign a contract or upload your book.

How do you evaluate author services?

Many authors want to use partnership companies to help manage the editing, cover design, publishing and marketing for their books. There is money to be made in the publishing industry and new companies spring up every month.

Some offer great service and value for money, others are sharks with expensive services that may leave you disappointed and out of pocket. The author community usually picks up on these pretty quickly, and you can easily find reputable services with good testimonials.

If a company is a Partner Member of the Alliance of Independent Authors, they have been evaluated and you can trust they have a good service.

For more detail, check out *Choose the Best Self-Publishing Services: ALLi's Guide to Assembling Your Tools and Your Team* by John Doppler and the Alliance of Independent Authors.

The money side of being an indie author

If you go indie, you'll need to pay for professional editing and book cover design before you publish. You can find free and cheap options, but if you want to make money from your books, you will need to invest.

Mark Dawson, bestselling author of the John Milton thriller series, says,

"Treat your writing as a business. Your books will be on a virtual shelf with the books of traditional authors, and you'll need to make sure that they can stand the inevitable comparison that readers will make. They don't care who publishes the books they read, but they do care that the cover looks professional, the blurb offers the promise of a fun read, and, once they start that read, they want the experience to be enjoyable (no typos, etc.).

You don't have to spend anything to get your books on Amazon, but that doesn't mean that you shouldn't. A small investment in your product will stand you in good stead."

Costs will vary depending on your experience and requirements. For example, a first-time fantasy author with a 150,000 word manuscript will spend more on editing than an experienced business consultant writing their third non-fiction book of 50,000 words.

Once you have your finished book, it is free to publish on the major digital platforms like Amazon KDP for ebook and print, Kobo Writing Life, Apple Books, Nook, and Google Play, as well as distributors like Draft2Digital, and audio platforms like ACX and Findaway Voices. All these services take a cut of sales. There is a small cost to publish on print distributor Ingram Spark, and PublishDrive has an upfront payment model instead of a royalty share. Check the platform terms and conditions as they change over time.

Each of these services pays by direct bank transfer or PayPal 60-90 days after the end of the month of sale: for example, you are paid for October's sales at the end of December. There are reporting dashboards on all services so you can track the volume of sales, revenue, and the impact of promotions and marketing.

Many indie authors spend some of their revenue on marketing activities, which is an important part of any business. More details in section 1.10.

Questions:

- What's the difference between self-publishing and becoming an indie author?

- What are the benefits of being an indie author?

- What are the downsides?

- How does the money work?

- Are you considering this route to publication? What are your reasons? What is your definition of success?

- How will you find recommended freelancers and services to work with?

- What do you need to take the next step?

Resources:

- *Successful Self-Publishing: How to Self-Publish and Market Your Book* — Joanna Penn

- *Your Author Business Plan: Take Your Author Career to the Next Level* — Joanna Penn

- *Creative Self-Publishing: Make and Sell Your Books Your Way* — Orna A. Ross and the Alliance of Independent Authors

- *An Author's Guide to Working with Libraries and Bookstores* — Mark Leslie Lefebvre

- *Winning Shelf Space: How to Get Your Self-Published Book into Bookstores* — Debbie Young, Orna A. Ross, and the Alliance of Independent Authors

- *Choose the Best Self-Publishing Services: ALLi's Guide to Assembling Your Tools and Your Team* — John Doppler and the Alliance of Independent Authors

- *Wide for the Win: Strategies to Sell Globally via Multiple Platforms and Forge Your Own Path to Success* — Mark Leslie Lefebvre

- WMG Writer's Guides by Dean Wesley Smith and Kristine Kathryn Rusch — WMGPublishinginc.com/writers

- Downloadable chart with spectrum of publishing possibilities by Jane Friedman — TheCreativePenn.com/publishingpaths

- List of editors — TheCreativePenn.com/editors

- List of book cover designers — TheCreativePenn.com/bookcoverdesign

- List of formatting options — TheCreativePenn.com/formatting

- List of useful tools — TheCreativePenn.com/tools

- Alliance of Independent Authors Watchdog listing — SelfPublishingAdvice.org/best-self-publishing-services

- Alliance of Independent Authors — AllianceIndependentAuthors.org

- Alliance of Independent Authors blog and podcast — SelfPublishingAdvice.org

- Mark Dawson's Self-Publishing Formula 101 Course — www.TheCreativePenn.com/101

- Wide for the Win Facebook group — Facebook.com/groups/wideforthewin

- 20BooksTo50K Facebook group — Facebook.com/groups/20Booksto50k

1.5 Write more books

You cannot make a living for the long term with just one book, however you choose to publish. One book with a great launch might have a spike of sales initially but over time the numbers will shrink, unless another book comes along to boost the signal.

Look at the Forbes Richest Author List and you'll find that the wealthiest traditionally published authors like James Patterson, Nora Roberts, and Stephen King all have a lot of books.

In the independent author community, the Facebook group 20BooksTo50K is based on the principle that 20 books will make an income of around US$50,000 annually, and that has proven true for many authors. That number may sound daunting to the new writer, but if you love writing, and you assume a hybrid approach to publishing, it's certainly possible.

The good news is that the more books you have, the less you have to market them because you'll have an audience ready and waiting, a critical mass of product on the digital shelves, and multiple streams of income.

As you write more books, you will also become a better writer and that means you can write faster and satisfy your audience — which in turn leads to more book sales. It all compounds over time.

Travel writer and podcaster Jeremy Bassetti says, "Writers who want to make a living with their writing must produce a fair amount of high-value intellectual property. The more works you have, the more visible you will be, and the more potential you will have to make a living. The principle is similar to compounding interest.

Producing high-value work is especially important when lower-value opportunities and entire industries disappear in the blink of an eye, as we have experienced with the coronavirus pandemic. Streams of income are like actual streams of water. Some are seasonal, drying up in the summer months, freezing in the winter months, and flooding in the spring."

Here are some ways you can write more books.

Improve your productivity

Every professional author has some kind of regular process to produce words on the page. Books don't magically appear. You need to schedule time to create them.

Identify your most creative period in the day and schedule that time to write. You have to find time from somewhere. Go through your schedule, book in your writing time and then turn up for that appointment with yourself.

I use Google Calendar and add writing time slots on weekday mornings for writing and editing. I had a day job for the first five years of my author career and I wrote between 5 am and 6 am before work. While I have more time to create now, I still write in the mornings.

Once I'm at my laptop ready for my writing session, I put on noise-cancelling headphones and play rain and thunderstorms to shut out the world. You will find your own way to get into the flow of writing, but definitely shut off your notifications and stay away from email and social media. You're here to write, everything else can wait!

For more writing productivity tips, check out *Productivity for Authors*.

Use tools to help you

There are a few key tools that can help you write more books. I use Scrivener software to keep track of ideas and research, structure and plan the content, write the first draft and edit. I also use ProWritingAid to self-edit and improve the book as much as I can before working with my editor.

I use Google Calendar to organize appointments and schedule my time, and the Things app (Mac only) for my To Do list.

Some authors use dictation to increase their word count per writing session. I have dictated some of my books, and as speech to text tools improve, I expect to do more of this. Most computers and phones now have built-in options, or you can use a specialist app like Dragon Anywhere.

You can find more tips on dictation and interviews with authors who dictate at TheCreativePenn.com/dictation

Write a series

Writing a series is a great way to speed up the writing process, satisfy your readers, and make more money, because customers will often buy more than one book. It's also easier to promote a series because you can set pricing deals on book one and still make a profit on the sale of multiple books.

For fiction authors, once you determine your series characters and world, you only have to come up with a new plot for each book. My ARKANE series has 11 books at the time of writing, and I have two other trilogies.

For non-fiction, you can create a series around a target audience or a theme, for example, I have Books for Writers.

All the publishing platforms enable you to add a series name which groups books together and aids discoverability. Some stores have a series page so readers can see which ones they've bought.

Award-winning author of equestrian fiction Natalie Keller Reinert says, "Writing in series and finding a unique, personal spin on a niche genre is the best way, in my opinion, to create longevity. I have been publishing and selling successfully for ten years by writing for an underserved market with a unique subject matter. It has given me very loyal readers, and also allows me to fine-tune my social media marketing in very precise ways."

> For more on writing a series, check out my interview with prolific fantasy author, Lindsay Buroker at TheCreativePenn.com/writeseries

Write non-fiction

There are many benefits to writing non-fiction, even if you're primarily a fiction author. It's easier to market as readers are looking for specific keywords which are usually in the title or sub-title. Non-fiction books often sell in multiple formats, for example, I listen to a lot of non-fiction audiobooks and I buy the ones I want to keep in hardback as well.

Non-fiction books can be more profitable as readers are less price-sensitive. They value the information and ideas and don't care so much about length. You can write a short non-fiction book and still charge premium prices, and full-length non-fiction often sells for more than fiction.

You can also turn non-fiction into other streams of income, for example, workbook editions or online courses, covered in more detail in later chapters.

If you write fiction, consider non-fiction related to your research. Fantasy author Neil Gaiman wrote *Norse Mythology*, whose myths underpin many of his novels. Scottish crime writer, Val McDermid, wrote *Forensics: The Anatomy of Crime*, about the science behind her stories. Literary fiction author, Roz Morris, wrote the memoir, *Not Quite Lost: Travels Without a Sense of Direction*, about the places that spark her novels.

You can also write helpful books for the author niche and many of the top writing books are written by fiction authors. *On Writing: A Memoir of the Craft* by Stephen King is one of my favorites and I recommend all the non-fiction books written by Dean Wesley Smith and Kristine Kathryn Rusch published under WMG Writer's Guides.

If you want to keep your author brand and audience separate, then consider using different names for your non-fiction, as I do with Joanna Penn and J.F. Penn.

More information and ideas in *How To Write Non-Fiction: Turn Your Knowledge into Words*.

Write short stories, novellas and other shorter works

There are genre conventions on the length of a book. 50,000-150,000 is the approximate range, but you can also write shorter works to earn more income and reach more readers.

Short stories can introduce new readers to your work, enable you to play with different creative ideas, and bring in income in multiple ways. You can license them to a primary market and once the rights revert, use them in anthologies and boxsets and as marketing on your website or in your email list. Novellas are slightly longer fiction works which you can use in a similar way.

For ideas around making money with short fiction, check out my interview with award-winning author, Douglas Smith, at TheCreativePenn.com/shortfiction

For non-fiction authors, multiple shorter books can be useful to your audience, easier to write, and more profitable than a longer book on a particular topic.

Co-write with other authors

Co-writing and collaboration have many creative benefits in terms of writing faster, coming up with ideas, and splitting the workload around editing and marketing. When I co-wrote the dark fantasy thriller, *Risen Gods*, with J. Thorn, we were both thrilled to finish the first draft in 19 days, many times faster than either of us had written a story alone.

It's also beneficial if both parties bring something different to the collaboration. I co-wrote *The Healthy Author* with Dr Euan Lawson, whose medical expertise alongside my anecdotal evidence and reach in the author community enabled a successful outcome for us both and a book that could not have existed if either of us had tried it alone.

Some fiction authors write in the same universe, with Michael Anderle and Craig Martelle sharing the success of this model in the 20BooksTo50K Facebook group.

With tools like automatic payment-splitting through Draft2Digital, it's easier than ever to collaborate with other authors, but be sure to sign an author agreement that makes the relationship clear and defines terms of copyright and payment.

For more detail, check out *Co-writing a Book: Collaboration and Co-creation for Writers.*

Make more of your backlist

A book is new to the reader who has just found it, so don't underestimate the power of your backlist. You can add new covers, change up the sales description, relaunch with a new marketing campaign, or even change categories if appropriate to reach a new readership.

Sweet romance and YA author Kat Bellemore says, "Your backlist is your moneymaker, so don't ignore your older books. Even though new releases can be an important part of your strategy to become a full-time author, if you don't have the best release, it's not going to break you. I have my new releases up for pre-order and tell my newsletter. I use paid newsletters for the first book in my series. But that's it. Focus on your backlist. Get it everywhere you can, in every medium you can."

Questions:

- How could you write and produce more books?

- What is stopping you from writing more books?

- How can you break through those blocks?

Resources:

- *Productivity for Authors: Find Time to Write, Organize Your Author Life, and Decide What Really Matters* — Joanna Penn

- *How To Write Non-Fiction: Turn Your Knowledge into Words* — Joanna Penn

- *Playing the Short Game: How to Market and Sell Short Fiction* — Douglas Smith

- *Taking the Short Tack: Creating Income and Connecting with Readers Using Short Fiction* — Matty Dalrymple

- *Co-writing a Book: Collaboration and Co-creation for Writers* — Joanna Penn and J. Thorn

- WMG Writer's Guides by Dean Wesley Smith and Kristine Kathryn Rusch — WMGPublishinginc.com/writers

- Scrivener software for writing — www.TheCreativePenn.com/scrivenersoftware

- ProWritingAid for editing — www.TheCreativePenn.com/prowritingaid

- Resources and interviews on dictation — www.TheCreativePenn.com/dictation

- Interview with prolific fantasy author Lindsay Buroker on writing a series — www.TheCreativePenn.com/writeseries

- Interview on making money with short fiction with award-winning author Douglas Smith at TheCreativePenn.com/shortfiction

1.6 Write books that people want to buy

In the last chapter, we considered how to write more books, but there's no point in writing so many if no one wants to buy them.

Most of us start out by writing the book of our hearts, the book we are truly driven to write. It's important for your creative integrity and I certainly did that with my first non-fiction book and many of my novels.

But if you want to make a living with your writing, you also have to consider what people might want to buy. You need to change your mindset: writing is about you, but the book is about the reader.

The ideal approach is to find the intersection of what you love to read and write and what readers are looking for. Here are some ways to figure out where the intersection might be for you.

Consider genre or category

You need to know what genre or category your book fits in however you choose to publish, so it's worth doing your research early in the process.

Find at least ten comparison books and/or authors, often referred to as 'comps,' and check which categories they're in on Amazon, or whichever store you prefer to shop on. Find the book and scroll down to check the categories.

This is usually obvious for non-fiction as categories relate to topics, for example, this book sits within Authorship as well as Writing Reference, and Small Business.

Fiction can be more complicated, as the book may span multiple genres, for example, my ARKANE thrillers encompass Action Adventure, Conspiracy Thriller, and Supernatural Thriller.

Check the rankings of the top books per sub-category to see what kind of book does well. Examine the covers and titles, as well as the sales description. What are the reader expectations for these types of books? What do the top-selling books have in common? How does your book fit alongside them?

> You can use a tool like Publisher Rocket to discover the categories that books are in as well as research other options to target. Find it at:
>
> TheCreativePenn.com/rocket
>
> For more help with genre and categories, check out the reports from K-lytics at:
>
> TheCreativePenn.com/genre

Consider search terms

People want a book for entertainment, information or inspiration. If a reader knows your name, they may search for your book directly, but it's more likely to be discovered by new readers if it answers someone's question, helps them to solve a problem, or fits their favorite genre or search criteria.

Readers browse their favorite category for books, but they also use the search bar to find what they want. They type in keyword phrases into Amazon, Google, or their favorite bookstore and see what comes up.

Amazon is a search engine for people who are actively ready to buy, so you definitely want your book to come up in relevant searches. This is why my non-fiction books have very obvious titles, but I learned the hard way!

Back in 2008, I published my first book, *How to Enjoy Your Job or Find a New One*. I knew nothing about search engine optimization (SEO) at the time.

In 2012, I rewrote the book and re-titled it as *Career Change* based on a keyword phrase with ten times the number of monthly searches. The book usually ranks on the first page of Amazon for the search term 'career change,' so people find it even though I don't do any specific marketing for that book and it doesn't relate to my other non-fiction titles.

Keywords are also important for fiction, for example, 'werewolf shifter romance,' or 'cozy British village mysteries.' Readers are pretty specific in their interests, and researching keywords might give you some more ideas for other books to write.

I use Publisher Rocket to research keywords. There's a free tutorial at TheCreativePenn.com/rocketkeywords

Ask your readers

Romance author Jessie Clever says, "I make a living salary from just book sales. I was able to do this because I targeted exactly what the readers in my genre want and then I wrote it. It sounds like it shouldn't be that simple, but it is. I've been self-publishing for seven years, and when I pivoted my business to truly focus on what the reader wanted, my sales took off."

While writing to market is an effective approach, you also need to write what you love or it won't be sustainable for the long term. Jessie Clever continues, "I love writing romance novels. There is no other story that allows me to play with the full wheel of emotions like a love story. Every book I write pulls at every emotion, pushes at every boundary, and always ends up being my new favorite book."

Readers will know if you don't truly love the genre you write and it won't be fun for you either. There are easier ways to make money than writing books, so make sure it's a fun living, not just an income!

Romance author Sadie King says, "Give your readers what they want! I think of myself as an entertainer and my purpose is to provide a short escape from everyday life, which has been especially true in the last twelve months due to the pandemic. I survey my email list to ask what they want me to write about, and if my readers want to read about firemen and curvy women, (which is what they wanted in my last survey) then that's what I'll give them! Oh, and have fun. Writing should be fun — painful at times — but mostly fun."

The best approach is to consider what you love to read and what you want to write and then research how to position that in a genre or category so you can reach those readers. How can you write at the intersection of what people love to read and what you love to write?

Questions:

- How can you make sure that there is an audience for your book?

- Who are your 'comp' authors and/or specific books?

- What are the reader expectations for these types of books?

- What do the top-selling books have in common? How does your book fit alongside them?

- What sub-categories are they in?

- What keywords might be relevant?

- How could you combine writing what you love with writing what people want to buy?

Resources:

- Publisher Rocket for keywords and categories — www.TheCreativePenn.com/rocket

- Free tutorial on researching keywords — TheCreativePenn.com/rocketkeywords

- Genre and category research reports at K-lytics — TheCreativePenn.com/genre

- *Write To Market: Deliver a Book That Sells* — Chris Fox

1.7 Publish in multiple formats

"Write and publish as frequently as you can create quality books, and publish in all formats (print, ebook, audio). Find what works: what your audience likes, and what sells best. Do more of that."

Holly Worton, Nature and adventure mindset author

Readers have preferences on book format.

The way you read is not necessarily the same as how other people read, so don't dismiss a format just because you don't use it yourself. If your work is available in multiple formats, you can reach every reader in their preferred way and bring in other streams of income from the same material.

These days, I read fiction in ebook format on my Kindle and occasionally listen to a novel as an audiobook, whereas for non-fiction, I prefer audiobook and will often buy the hardback or paperback if I want to review the content later. I also buy a lot of non-fiction in print for book research purposes.

I release my own books in ebook, paperback, hardback, large print and audiobook editions, as well as some workbooks, under my Curl Up Press imprint. Print-on-demand makes it easier and much cheaper to release multiple print editions.

Here are some format possibilities and you can find detail on how to publish them in my free ebook, *Successful Self-Publishing,* also available in print and audio.

Ebook

The ebook market is increasingly fragmented and you can reach readers in 190 countries if you publish your ebooks on the various platforms. The biggest retailers include Amazon Kindle, Apple Books, Kobo, Nook, and Google Play, but there are also many more services across the world, as well as library ebook distribution, which expanded significantly during the pandemic.

You can publish direct and/or use aggregators like Draft-2Digital, Smashwords, PublishDrive, or Streetlib for distribution.

You can easily format your ebooks with Vellum for all stores, and I have a tutorial on how to format an ebook and a print book. You can find more options for formatting at TheCreativePenn.com/formatting

Paperback

You can publish print-on-demand paperbacks in various sizes through KDP Print and Ingram Spark. Most independent authors now use both services, using KDP Print for Amazon only, and Ingram Spark for wide distribution which enables discounting, optional returns, and ease of ordering for bookstores, libraries, universities, and online retailers.

Large print (paperback or hardback)

Many readers want to read print books but find the font size in many of them too small. Large print books are not usually for sale in physical bookstores, so they are an underserved market with an audience who purchase online or borrow from libraries. They are easy to produce with print-on-demand.

Large print books can be particularly popular with certain demographics. My mum writes sweet romance as Penny Appleton and in 2020, 55% of her book sales income came from large print editions. I don't sell as many with my two main brands, but with print-on-demand, there's very little upfront cost so I have some available, anyway.

I create paperback large print editions but some authors have found that hardback large print can also be worth doing, as libraries prefer them and they make lovely gifts.

Audiobook

Audiobooks are the fastest growing segment in publishing, with an expanding range of options for global distribution. You can reach listeners through 42 different platforms including Audible, Apple Books, and Google Play, as well as subscription sites like Storytel and Scribd, and library services if you publish through ACX and Findaway Voices.

For more detail on producing, publishing and marketing audiobooks, check out *Audio for Authors: Audiobooks, Podcasting, and Voice Technologies.*

Hardback

You can publish print-on-demand hardback editions through Ingram Spark with options for case laminate, cloth, or dust jacket cover.

Workbooks

If you write non-fiction and/or teach workshops, work-books can be a good option to add another product.

I create 6 x 9 inch paperbacks which include questions from the book and lines for people to write in the answers. There's a workbook that goes along with this book if you'd like to try it at:

TheCreativePenn.com/makealivingworkbook

Ebook boxsets or bundling

Ebook boxsets are great value for readers and enable the binge consumption that many prefer. They are sometimes called omnibus editions and while there is no physical box, the cover makes it clear that there are multiple books included.

They are easy to advertise at a special price, and this kind of boxset promotion can help you to hit significant bestseller lists. For example, my thriller, *One Day in Budapest*, was in the Deadly Dozen Boxset, which hit the New York Times bestseller list in 2014 and sold over 110,000 copies. I also hit the USA Today bestseller list with my ARKANE three-book boxset in 2016, five years after I published the first book in the series.

Ebook boxsets are more common for fiction authors with a series. For example, I have three ARKANE boxsets containing three ebooks each, as well as a nine-book boxset. You can create non-fiction boxsets around a theme or produce a multi-author boxset promotion.

Many authors worry about the boxset edition cannibalizing sales of individual books, but I've found boxset readers differ from those who prefer single book reading. If you don't have ebook boxsets, you're definitely missing out on income and promotional opportunities.

You can easily create ebook boxsets with Vellum.

Audiobook boxsets

Audiobook boxsets offer the same benefits as ebook boxsets. They are particularly good value for listeners who buy credits on sites like Audible and enable authors with shorter books to compete with longer fiction works as listeners want the best value for their credit.

Special editions

Special editions can't be produced with print-on-demand as they are usually a limited print run with special features like special paper, leather bindings, or gold embossing on the cover.

They require upfront payment for specialist design and printing, and then the books must be warehoused and shipped to the customer which takes time and more money, so this type of project is only for those authors who have the budget and professional help with production.

Some authors use crowdfunding for these special projects, as covered further in section 2.3. For example, author and poet Orna Ross created a limited-edition, gold-embossed hardback with a custom design for *Secret Rose* to mark the 150th anniversary of the birth of W.B. Yeats.

Traditionally published authors can also create these kinds of projects if they retain the rights. Fantasy author Brandon Sanderson raised nearly US$7 million on Kickstarter to create the 10th anniversary leather-bound edition of *The Way of Kings* in 2020. Although he licenses most of his rights to publishers, he retained special editions. Certainly something to consider if you're signing a contract with a publisher.

Bulk sales

Bulk sales, also known as direct or corporate or special sales, involve selling hundreds or even thousands of books at once to a specific organization. They order and pay in advance, then the books are printed and delivered. These sales have no impact on metrics like ranking on bestseller lists, but they do put money directly in your pocket!

Canadian author David Chilton, known as *The Wealthy Barber*, has made hundreds of thousands of dollars selling his finance books in bulk to large corporates. In an interview on The Creative Penn Podcast, David said, "I've never seen a better Return On Investment on efforts than I see in the corporate sales arena of the book publishing industry."

This approach can also be used for sales to schools. Author David Hendrickson's YA novels feature bullying and other topics that schools want to discuss in class. He sells books in bulk directly to schools for use in lessons, printing them through Ingram Spark.

Questions:

- What formats do you read?
- What formats are your books available in right now?
- What other formats could you create? (If you retain the rights)

Resources:

- *Successful Self-Publishing: How to Self-Publish and Market Your Book* — Joanna Penn

- *Creative Self-Publishing: Make and Sell Your Books Your Way* — Orna A. Ross and the Alliance of Independent Authors

- *An Author's Guide to Working with Libraries & Bookstores* — Mark Leslie Lefebvre

- *Audio for Authors: Audiobooks, Podcasting, and Voice Technologies* — Joanna Penn

- *How to Make Real Money Selling Books without Worrying about Returns* — Brian Jud

- *How to Get Your Book Into Schools and Double Your Income With Volume Sales* — David H. Hendrickson

- Formatting options including software and free-lancers — www.TheCreativePenn.com/formatting

- Vellum software for ebook and print formatting — www.TheCreativePenn.com/vellum

- Tutorial on how to use Vellum for formatting — www.TheCreativePenn.com/vellum-tutorial

- Interview with David Chilton on bulk sales — www.TheCreativePenn.com/davidchilton

- David Chilton's course on bulk sales — www.TheCreativePenn.com/bulksales

- Interview with David Hendrickson on selling directly into schools — www.TheCreativePenn.com/schoolsales

1.8 Publish globally

Many authors dream of seeing their book in a physical bookstore in their area. While that is one definition of success, there is a much bigger global market of readers out there who might want your book.

Is your book available in English?

English is the most international language, and it's spoken — and read — in almost every country on earth.

For example, there are more English speakers in India, Pakistan, Nigeria, or the Philippines than there are in the UK, and many of these are educated, middle-class readers who might want your book. With mobile penetration increasing every year, and more readers on mobile apps, the opportunities for discovery and book sales continue to rise.

Back in 2012, I had only sold books in English in 6 countries, rising to 49 in 2015, and 162 by early 2021. Most independent authors make the bulk of their income from the US, UK, Australia and Canada, but the percentage of income from other countries is rising, and will continue to do so as other digital markets mature, accelerated by the pandemic.

How do you know if you have particular international rights to your work?

The traditional publishing industry is divided into territories, and most agents and publishers will have a primary area, for example, North America or UK Commonwealth, while they may also partner with agents and publishers for foreign rights licensing in other territories and languages. Your contract will specify licensing by territory, language, and format as well as length of time and other terms.

If you have a traditional publishing deal for some of those formats or territories, you might also be able to self-publish in other countries or in other formats or languages and make more from your intellectual property.

Independent authors who retain all their rights can publish in 190 countries for ebooks and a smaller number with other formats through the main platforms, most of which cover multiple languages. Some indie authors also work with agents and publishers for foreign rights licensing, as covered in section 1.1.

Did you sign a contract for your book or other written work with an agent or publisher? If yes, find your contract and check which formats and languages you licensed for which territories.

If you're an independent author, have you signed any kind of exclusivity agreement, for example, KDP Select for ebooks or ACX, for exclusive terms? If you work with an author services company, you should also check your contract.

If you're like me, and generally publish wide with every book and every format, then you're good to go!

Are your books available in as many countries as possible on as many stores as possible in as many formats as possible?

We live in an increasingly digital market where a reader on the other side of the world could hear about your book through a podcast interview or a social media post or an online article. If a reader can hear about your book, then they should also be able to buy it or borrow it from the library or download it as part of their subscription service.

Readers are generally wonderful and they want to support authors and creators, but if your book is not available easily and legally in their country, then readers may resort to piracy, or they may just forget about you and read a book that is available.

If you publish wide, as covered in section 1.4 on self-publishing, your books can be available in 190 countries for ebooks, and many of those for print-on-demand and audiobooks, with more opportunities for distribution arriving all the time.

Make sure your pricing is appropriate. Check other books in your genre on the country stores and set local pricing in your self-publishing dashboard on the various services. Reedsy has a free course on pricing books for an international market if you're unclear on how to do this.

Are your books available in libraries in ebook, audiobook, and print?

The pandemic accelerated the adoption of ebooks and audiobooks in libraries, and independent authors can offer great value through the cost-per-checkout model. Your books are free to the reader and you still get paid. It's a win-win! Some countries, like the UK and Canada, also have licensing and collection services which provide extra revenue, covered further in section 2.11.

Libraries use various services by territory, for example, Overdrive reaches readers across North America, Europe, and Asia Pacific.

You can reach libraries with your ebooks through Draft-2Digital, Smashwords, and PublishDrive, and also Overdrive specifically through Kobo Writing Life. You can reach libraries with your audiobooks through Findaway Voices, and if your print books are available through Ingram Spark, they will be available in library catalogs.

> For more on libraries, check out *An Author's Guide to Working with Libraries and Bookstores* by Mark Leslie Lefebvre.

License to publishers in foreign languages and/or other territories

If you're traditionally published and have licensed foreign rights, your agent or publisher will manage that side of things.

Independent authors can also license foreign rights and many successful indies are approached by publishing companies looking to license books, while others work with agents to specifically license foreign rights.

For example, children's author, Karen Inglis, licensed her book, *The Secret Lake*, to publishers in Russia, Turkey, Albania, the Czech Republic, China, Iran, and Ukraine. All approached her after the book's success on Amazon in English, which she drove with Amazon Ads. She has also self-published the book in German.

The Alliance of Independent Authors recommends guiding principles for rights licensing including: Understand the contract, capitalize on as many rights as possible, limit the term, territory and formats, do your research, and strategize your sales efforts.

Self-publishing in translation

You can self-publish in translation and if you're bilingual, this can be a great way to expand your income streams, especially as new language markets emerge.

As Ricardo Fayet from Reedsy noted on Written Word Media in January 2021, "One thing the pandemic has greatly developed is the eBook market in European countries that were previously viewed as extremely traditional in their book-buying habits. Whatever the evolution of the pandemic, I can only see this trend further developing. I'd recommend going for the German market first, but I feel the French, Italian and Spanish ones will be catching up quickly."

Artificial Intelligence tools like Deepl.com can help with generating the first draft, especially for non-fiction books, but you will still need to work with an editor and proofreader to ensure your book is a quality product. I have three non-fiction books in German created through this method, with more on the way. I use Amazon auto-ads for marketing, and the books remain profitable. You can find more details at TheCreativePenn.com/AIGerman.

Award-winning paranormal romance author Nadine Mutas says, "Translation sales make up more than half of my income. I don't license my foreign rights, but I publish translations myself. I hire translators (German, Italian, and French) and then manage the publication direct on the retailers as I do my English books."

This is definitely an advanced option for authors who have the time and budget to spend on quality translation and marketing. You can find translators through the Reedsy Marketplace and also through professional translation associations such as the International Association of Professional Translators and Interpreters, or the Institute of Translation and Interpreting.

How do you market your books globally?

Almost all online content marketing is international. If you write an article online, or do a podcast interview, or use social media, people all over the world can find your words. For example, my Creative Penn Podcast has been downloaded in 223 countries.

You can also use country-specific paid advertising. Amazon has advertising options for eight countries at the time of writing, accessible from the KDP Dashboard. Kobo Writing Life has regular promotions by territory and BookBub offers international pay-per-click advertising. Facebook Ads can be targeted by country as well as interests, reading devices, and stores, and there are many other options emerging as digital markets expand.

Questions:

- Are your books available globally in English in ebook, paperback, and audiobook (if appropriate)?

- How can you expand your distribution to more global markets?

- Are you interested in foreign rights licensing? Would self-publishing in translation work for your author business?

- What are your next steps to take this further?

- How could you market your books to a global audience?

Resources:

- *Selective Rights Licensing: Sell your Book Rights at Home and Abroad* — Orna Ross and Helen Sedwick

- *An Author's Guide to Working with Libraries and Bookstores* — Mark Leslie Lefebvre

- *Wide for the Win: Strategies to Sell Globally via Multiple Platforms and Forge Your Own Path to Success* — Mark Leslie Lefebvre

- Self-publishing in Translation: Adventures with AI and German — TheCreativePenn.com/AIGerman

- Interview with Karen Inglis on her success with children's books — SelfPublishingFormula.com/episode-239

- Ultimate Guide to Rights Licensing from the Alliance of Independent Authors — SelfPublishingAdvice.org/rights-licensing-for-indie-authors

- International Association of Professional Translators and Interpreters — www.iapti.org

- Institute of Translation and Interpreting — www.iti.org.uk

- Reedsy Marketplace for translators — www.TheCreativePenn.com/reedsy

- Reedsy free course on international pricing — www.TheCreativePenn.com/internationalpricing

1.9 Sell direct to your audience

If you own and control your intellectual property rights, you can sell direct to your audience in multiple formats, as well as distributing your books through all the established vendors.

As Orna Ross says on the Alliance of Independent Authors' blog, selling direct "is the most important trend emerging for authors. Increased author confidence is coming together with other favorable conditions and consumer trends to make this possible now in a way that it wasn't before. The rise in the Maker Movement, in personal branding, in mindful consumption, in mobile phone sales and in new technologies are all pointing in this direction."

Benefits of selling direct

You receive a higher royalty on selling direct, usually 80-90% even after factoring in platform costs and bank fees. You also receive income in your bank or PayPal account within hours of payment, sometimes within minutes, compared to months or even years through publishing in other ways.

Some readers want to support authors and independent creators and understand that buying direct helps financially.

You can also reach readers across the world who might not have access to purchase on the other platforms, or those who don't want to transact on certain sites for ethical reasons.

When selling on existing platforms, you never know who buys your book. If you sell direct, you know who the reader is, although of course, you need to comply with anti-spam and data protection regulations like GDPR. You can integrate the platforms with your email service and market to readers directly without relying on the distributors.

You can also market to existing readers without having to rely on advertising, which eats into profits on the vendor platforms. As long as you have an email list, you can reach readers with an offer.

Selling direct is a great way to make income quickly by offering value to your audience. In the early days of the pandemic in 2020, anxiety was high, the stock market crashed, and we were all worried about making money in increasingly tough times. I emailed my list with a discounted offer to buy direct and made several thousand dollars within 24 hours, money that really helped in those first difficult months when everything felt out of control.

How to sell ebooks and audiobooks direct

There are different digital solutions for selling ebooks and audiobooks online, but make sure you investigate how they handle digital taxes. The EU has specific (painful) digital tax rules, and increasingly, other jurisdictions are adding them too.

I use Payhip to sell my ebooks and audiobooks, which integrates with Bookfunnel for delivery, as well as integrating with Stripe and PayPal for payment. Payhip manages EU digital taxes, enables promotional coupons and other marketing options. Bookfunnel delivers the ebook to the reader's preferred device and to the Bookfunnel app for audio. They also manage customer service and help readers to access the book if they have trouble.

For more detail, check out my tutorial at:

TheCreativePenn.com/selldirecttutorial

I also use AuthorsDirect through Findaway Voices for audio, although this is only available in specific territories at the time of writing.

Other options include WooCommerce, SELZ, Gumroad, Shopify, eJunkie, and Fastspring. Remember to check the tax options as you investigate further. The Alliance of Independent Authors has more details in The Ultimate Guide to Selling Books on your Author Website.

Downloadable PDFs

You can also sell downloadable PDFs, for example, white papers, guides, resources, handbooks, designs, patterns, recipes, and other material.

If you sell these on the book distribution sites, you're constrained by their existing pricing model where ebooks are usually 99c - $14.99. If you sell direct, you can set a higher price point. If people want your information and it's useful, they will pay more for the download.

Sell print books direct

Many authors sell print books at conferences, conventions, workshops, readings, speaking events, or even local markets. You can purchase your books in bulk from your publisher or buy from Ingram Spark or other printers, then sell for a profit.

You can also sell print books directly to readers from your website or sites like Etsy or eBay, but most authors only do this for a small volume of signed copies for super fans or as a marketing activity. You have to manage stock, storage, and shipping so it can be expensive and time-consuming.

If you want to sell print directly, you can use something as simple as a PayPal button on your website. You can also use Payhip and some other digital options for physical products, or more extensive solutions with options for drop shipping through Shopify.

Adventure travel author Alastair Humphreys uses the WooCommerce plugin on his website, and social enterprise EnabledWorks.co.uk for storage and fulfillment.

If you publish print books through Ingram Spark, you can also use Aer.io to create an online store for your print-on-demand books, or use Bookshop.org for a curated bookshelf of your books. Both of these services are territory-specific.

Should you sell direct?

Even though you can make higher royalties selling direct, there are monthly fees for each of the services, so you need to make a certain amount per month to cover those costs. If you're a new author with just a couple of books and no email list, it won't be worth it until you've grown your backlist and your audience.

If you care about ranking on the online stores, then selling direct is not for you either. No one sees your direct sales and they don't count toward any bestseller lists.

If you're more established with a number of books that you have the rights to distribute, and an email list to reach people with your promotions, and you care more about money in your bank account than ranking, then selling direct might be worth doing. Only you can assess the potential for your situation.

How can you sell more books through direct channels?

I mainly sell books direct by telling my audience about it, as I am doing here in my books and on my podcast. Link to buy direct from your book pages, and offer discounts for readers to buy direct on your email list and through your books.

If you want to try the process as a customer, you can download *Successful Self-Publishing* for free in ebook and audiobook format at:

Payhip.com/thecreativepenn

You can also use coupon: LIVING to get 25% off any of my ebooks and audiobooks. If the process is unclear, check out:

TheCreativePenn.com/payhip-coupon

Questions:

- What are the benefits of selling direct, both for the customer and for you?

- How could you sell direct from your website?

- What do you need to have in place to make this worthwhile? If you're not at that point yet, how can you move in that direction?

Resources:

- Payhip for selling ebooks and audiobooks direct — www.TheCreativePenn.com/payhip

- Buy ebooks and audiobooks directly from me — www.Payhip.com/thecreativepenn

- Process of using a Payhip coupon — www.TheCreativePenn.com/payhip-coupon

- Bookfunnel for delivery of ebooks and audiobooks — www.TheCreativePenn.com/bookfunnel

- My tutorial on selling ebooks and audiobooks direct with Payhip and Bookfunnel — www.TheCreativePenn.com/selldirecttutorial

- The Ultimate Guide to Selling Books on your Author Website by the Alliance of Independent Authors — SelfPublishingAdvice.org/selling-books-on-your-author-website

1.10 Market your books

You cannot publish a book and just expect it to sell. That's not the reality of life in the 2020s, regardless of whether you go the traditional or indie route.

There are so many millions of books and a multitude of other options for consumers including TV, film, gaming, music and podcasts. You need to draw attention to your work somehow.

Marketing is the act of promoting your books, products, or services and although many authors resist it, marketing is an integral part of the writing life and therefore critical if you want to make a living this way.

There are lots of different ways to market your books and build your author platform, which I cover extensively in *How to Market a Book*, so this is just an introduction.

Marketing is a mindset

Most authors don't even want to think about marketing but it will be easier, and perhaps even fun, if you change your mindset.

Marketing is sharing what you love with people who will appreciate hearing about it. It doesn't have to be scammy or sucky, or forcibly ramming your book down people's throats in real life or on social media.

Think about your audience and consider how you might serve them through entertainment, education, or inspiration, then work out the best way to reach them in ways that also leave you creatively satisfied. You have a great book, so how can you make sure your target market have a chance to read it?

Marketing is a skill

You can learn marketing in the same way that you can learn writing or business skills. You just have to want to do it. Keep an open mind about what you might enjoy or what might work for your book/s and try different things.

I started podcasting in 2009 because I felt isolated and I wanted to talk to other authors around the world as well as learn and share tips about the writer's journey. I really didn't know what I was doing and for the first interview, I held an MP3 recorder next to the phone which I put on speaker. Yes, this was an actual landline, back in the days before Skype and Zoom went mainstream and way before podcasting became big enough to attract useful services.

But at least I started, and over a decade later, I have two podcasts which form the basis of my book marketing, and which provide other income streams which I cover in Part 2. I love podcasting and I consider my shows to be part of my creative body of work, as well as bringing in money and selling books. I certainly didn't know what the future would hold when I recorded that first episode back in 2009, but I enjoyed the process, so I kept doing it!

Take care of the basics first

The basics of book marketing are simple, but not easy!

Write a great book and understand where it fits in the ecosystem so your book cover resonates with that audience. Ensure your book description draws people in and use appropriate categories and keywords so your book can be found in the stores.

Set up a professional author website and email list so you can build your relationship with readers. Over time, you can use this list for launches, building an Advance Reader team, and for advertising.

Once you have these basics sorted, then you can consider the myriad other ways to market your books, but without these, you will find marketing difficult over the long term.

Use your books to market your books

If you have multiple books and you control your intellectual property, you can use different methods to sell more. Many fiction writers use free days in Kindle Unlimited, a free first in series if publishing wide, or at least periodic sale promotions, to drive more readers to the rest of the books.

My ARKANE thriller, *Stone of Fire*, has been free for many years on all stores and continues to bring people into the series of 11 books (and counting). I also have *Successful Self-Publishing* as a free first in series for non-fiction.

If you write in a series, regardless of genre, your books are linked together on the stores, which helps people to find them, and you can list all your books in the back matter so people are aware of them.

You can also bump up your backlist by doing new covers, updating your sales descriptions and relaunching with price promotions and other marketing.

Market in a way that suits your personality and lifestyle

The most effective marketing involves long-term actions that, over time, build up a readership that continues to bring you income and helps you to make a living with your writing. But if you want to do anything for the long term and enjoy it, it needs to be sustainable for your life.

Like diet or exercise, you can do anything for the short term, but if you hate it, you will soon fall off the wagon and might end up in a worse situation than before. So while you might try all kinds of different marketing tactics, settle on those that you enjoy and can do for the long term and ignore the rest.

I use the same methods for my fiction as J.F. Penn and non-fiction as Joanna Penn. These have developed over more than a decade, so don't worry, you don't need to have everything in place when you're starting out. I've tried pretty much everything over the years, but I've settled on these methods as they work well for me. Your preferences will probably differ.

I use content marketing through my two podcasts, The Creative Penn and Books and Travel, which also have transcripts and images on the show notes for effective search engine optimization (SEO). The shows have a call to action to join my email lists.

I offer a free thriller at JFPenn.com/free and my Author Blueprint at: TheCreativePenn.com/blueprint

I have free ebooks on all the stores, *Stone of Fire*, ARKANE thriller book 1, and also *Successful Self-Publishing*, and I promote them both with paid advertising and email marketing. I'm no longer a heavy user of social media, preferring to rely on email marketing, podcasting, and paid ads, which I've found deliver a much better return on investment and are more sustainable for my lifestyle.

There are many marketing options, so you need to find what works for you, but be sure to revisit your choices and try new things over time.

Learn how to market your own books before outsourcing

Most authors don't want to do their own marketing, but if you outsource too soon, you will end up out of pocket. For example, I've seen authors with just one book pay a PR company thousands of dollars as a retainer, only to find they get one interview in a small magazine that results in few sales. Better to spend that budget on a professional book cover, email list set-up and some basic paid ads which will drive sales or at least free downloads which result in reviews, while you write the next book.

There are lots of books and courses on marketing by authors with experience. Learn the basics first and once you have enough books, and you're making enough revenue to justify outsourcing, then look for the best return on investment for your marketing spend.

You can find free courses on marketing and professionals to help you at the Reedsy Marketplace:

TheCreativePenn.com/reedsy

Questions:

- What is your current attitude to book marketing? How could you improve your mindset?

- If you have a book or more out already, do you have the basics in place?

- How could you use your books to market your books?

- What kinds of marketing are you interested in learning more about? What might work for your personality and lifestyle over the long term?

- How could you improve your marketing skills?

- When is a good time to outsource your marketing? Is it the right time for you?

Resources:

- *How to Market a Book* — Joanna Penn

- *Strangers to Superfans: A Marketing Guide to the Reader Journey* — David Gaughran

- *How to Market a Book: Over-perform in a Crowded Market* — Ricardo Fayet

- My author website tutorial — www.TheCreativePenn.com/authorwebsite

- My email list set-up tutorial — www.TheCreativePenn.com/setup-email-list

- 101 Course for Authors by Mark Dawson, including the basics you need in place for successful self-publishing — www.TheCreativePenn.com/101

- Ads for Authors course by Mark Dawson, including Facebook, Amazon, and BookBub Ads — www.TheCreativePenn.com/ads

- Your First 10K Readers course by Nick Stephenson — www.TheCreativePenn.com/10k

Part 2:
How to Make Money with your Writing in Other Ways

2.1 Your author ecosystem

In Part 1, we went through all the ways you can make money with books, and in Part 2, we'll consider some other ways that your writing can bring in multiple streams of income. But before we get into the detail, it's important to understand how developing an ecosystem can amplify your revenue streams if you focus on building for the long term.

What is an author ecosystem?

An ecosystem is basically a network, and in this context, it's all the things that work together to sell your books and bring in multiple streams of income in other ways.

If you build an ecosystem, it will become much easier to make money. It will all work together in the background, compounding over time as you continue to write and increase your body of work, and you should be able to track how each aspect feeds into your revenue streams.

My non-fiction ecosystem for Joanna Penn

The central hub is my website, TheCreativePenn.com. Since 2008, I've created articles, videos, and my podcast as content marketing to attract people to the site, as well as sharing on social media. Traffic to my website results in book sales, affiliate income, sales of my courses, and sign-ups to my email list through my Author Blueprint.

The Blueprint has an email series which in turn links back to my books, and to affiliate links, courses, and the podcast. The podcast brings in Patreon subscriptions, advertising revenue, and affiliate income, plus also sells my books and courses. Most of my paid speaking engagements have come from people finding me through my books and podcast, and if I needed to, I could easily turn on a consulting or coaching revenue stream by emailing my list.

On the book sites, my free ebook, *Successful Self-Publishing*, drives revenue through sales of the print and audiobook versions, as well as leading people into my other non-fiction books and courses, plus all my books contain affiliate links, and links to my other books and the podcast.

Everything links to everything else, so if I drive more traffic to my website or sales of my books through paid advertising, it amplifies the whole ecosystem and results in more streams of income.

Jo Parfitt, author of 30+ non-fiction books, says, "Spin whatever you create as many ways as you can. If it starts as a live workshop, turn it into a book, into an online course, a workshop, a residential course and then, of course, articles and blogs that become your marketing funnel. In other words: exploit yourself!"

My fiction ecosystem for J.F. Penn

The central hub is my website, JFPenn.com, which has pages for each of my books with links to the various stores and how to buy direct, as well as an email sign-up for my free thriller ebook at JFPenn.com/free.

The automated email series introduces readers to my books and after a period of time, includes an offer to be part of my Pennfriends team for Advanced Review Copies.

I have a permafree first in series, *Stone of Fire*, on all the ebook stores which is easy to advertise and brings people to my books. Some buy others in the 11-book series, or some of my other fiction, and some also sign up for my email list.

My Books and Travel Podcast has a call to action for the free thriller, and I mention my books as part of the content so people check out my fiction if they're interested. I'm also expanding into affiliate links for the BooksAndTravel.page website and I'm considering other revenue streams around the podcast, as well as non-fiction related to my research.

Design an ecosystem for the long term

This ecosystem approach will amplify almost all of the income streams in this book, so it's well worth considering for your situation. Jeff Elkins, The Dialogue Doctor, says, "I multiplied my income 10-fold in one year by opening new options for revenue. I was shocked at how those options built on each other. As the new options grew, the old ones grew as well."

Of course, if you're just starting out, it's hard to imagine a future state where everything amplifies in this way, but if you think about it strategically early on, you can build something that will grow and expand over time. As you go through the rest of the book, consider the various income streams and how they might amplify each other. This will make it easier to make money as your ecosystem grows.

If you're further into the author journey, consider what your ecosystem looks like right now. Is it integrated in multiple ways so that each part drives revenue?

Start with where you are and consider what you want your ecosystem to look like in five or ten years' time, and take action toward that.

Questions:

- How does an ecosystem work to drive revenue in multiple ways?

- What does your ecosystem look like now?

- If you carry on as you are for the next five years, or ten years, what will your ecosystem look like?

- What do you need to change to ensure it works for you over the long term?

Resources:

- *Your Author Business Plan: Take Your Author Career to the Next Level* — Joanna Penn

2.2 Affiliate income

Affiliate income is commission on sales that you make for someone else's product or service.

You don't have to manage customers yourself, you just drive traffic to their sales page, which makes it a truly scalable form of income. As your email list expands, as traffic to your website grows, as your books sell more, your affiliate revenue will rise as well.

It takes time, but if you are intending to have a long-term career, it can be well worth integrating as part of your streams of income. My first affiliate payment back in 2008 was $1.78 from Amazon Associates, hardly worth the effort of creating the links. But over a decade later, I make six figures annually from affiliate sales, so it's been well worth the time to grow and maintain.

Ethical (and successful) affiliate marketing

Trust and reputation are far more important than easy cash.

I only recommend products and services that I use personally and are useful to my audience. Although I am offered opportunities that would bring in immediate revenue if I promoted them, I would never risk the trust of my audience for the sake of short-term income.

If you're ethical with your affiliate recommendations and marketing, then your audience will thank you for sharing and help you by spreading the word. People *want* to buy things that will help them or entertain them. If we can be trusted advisors curating a sea of possibilities, then recommending affiliate products is a useful thing to do as well as a great income stream.

Serving your audience will also make you a more successful affiliate marketer. If you offer something that is a bad fit, no one will click on your link. If you recommend something that is low quality or a bad customer experience, or if you're not honest about being an affiliate, they will find out anyway and they won't trust your recommendation next time.

Start with your book links to the online vendors

Since you're already promoting your books on your website, in emails and on social media, you might as well make a few cents more by using an affiliate link.

Amazon Associates enables you to set up one link that redirects to various country stores and you receive a (tiny) percentage of whatever people buy on the site during a 24-hour period.

Apple's affiliate program enables you to link to songs and albums, audiobooks and books, films and TV shows and offers several tools to help design the right links and images.

Kobo's affiliate program is managed by owner e-commerce company, Rakuten, and you can promote other books and products outside of Kobo if you use their network.

Even online store, Bookshop.org, has its own affiliate program if you want to help independent booksellers.

You can also use a site like Booklinker.net or Books2Read.com to create one link that works for all stores and contains affiliate links. Books2Read also has the option of using a Facebook pixel for ad tracking.

Useful products, tools and services

Think about your niche and your specific audience. What might be useful for them?

My non-fiction audience are authors, so I offer things they need:

- Services like editing at: TheCreativePenn.com/ editors and cover design at: TheCreativePenn.com/bookcoverdesign

- Tools for writing, editing, publishing, and marketing at TheCreativePenn.com/tools

- Online courses at TheCreativePenn.com/courses

These offers could also be tangential, for example, if you write cat cozy mysteries, you could research cat-related products and/or services that you recommend on a page on your website with affiliate links, or even within the books themselves.

How do you become an affiliate?

If you already use a product or service, there might be details within the program with how you can promote it. Or you can Google the product or service and 'affiliate program' and you're likely to find information on how to enroll. If there is nothing publicly listed, then you could email the company and ask if they have an affiliate program.

You might need to show evidence of the size of your audience and have a plan for promotion. You're more likely to be approved if you have measurable traffic on your website, podcast downloads, or a substantial email list.

Check the terms and conditions. For example, many programs don't allow paid ads as they don't want competition driving higher ad prices.

Once you have your affiliate link, you need to drive traffic to it. Only a certain percentage will click through to buy, so you need ways to bring people into the funnel.

Here are some ideas.

Create a video tutorial

Demonstrate how people can use the product you recommend in a free video that is useful in its own right.

I have a free video tutorial series on how to build and set up your author website and email list at:

TheCreativePenn.com/authorwebsite

The videos contain affiliate links to different products and services, and I also give people options to go straight to the sites without using my links. I state clearly that I'm an affiliate and people don't need to use my links in order to get the benefit of the content. I just ask that people use my links if they find it useful.

I also create tutorials for the most useful software for authors, for example, how to format your ebook and print book using Vellum at:

TheCreativePenn.com/vellum-tutorial

Create a recommendation page

Include your affiliate links in one place on your website. I have a tools page at TheCreativePenn.com/tools and some people use 'Favorite Things' or 'Products I love.'

Use links in your books

This is easier for non-fiction authors, as you can easily integrate links within your books as I have within this one. I always include a notice in the first chapter which you're welcome to use as a template:

> *Note:* There are affiliate links within this book to products and services that I recommend and use personally. This means that I receive a small percentage of the sale at no extra cost to you, and in some cases, you may receive a discount for using my link. I only recommend products and services that I believe are great for authors, so I hope you find them useful.

I recommend using a URL shortener for your links, so it's easy for people to type into a browser from a print edition. I use Pretty Links plugin for WordPress, but there are other options. You can also offer a download page from your audiobook so that listeners can access the information as well.

This book has a download page at:

TheCreativePenn.com/makealivingdownload

Use links in your emails

Once you have an email list sign up on your site, you can include affiliate links in emails to your audience. For example, if you sign up to my Author Blueprint at TheCreativePenn.com/blueprint you'll get useful emails, articles, and videos, some of which contain my affiliate links.

I also email my list with updates and offers over time, and try to use at least one affiliate link in every email. Maintaining an email list costs money and you won't be selling books every time, so it's good to have other content and offers in order to make your list pay for itself.

Use links in your regular content

Whether you blog, podcast, make videos, and/or use social media, you will probably create content that is useful, entertaining and/or inspirational to bring people to your books.

Consider creating specific content that also attracts people to your affiliate links. For example, every author will need an editor at some point, so I made a video and article on how to find and work with professional editors which is useful on its own and leads people to my editors page, which includes some affiliate links and other useful resources.

Host joint venture webinars

Webinars are free, live online events with replays available afterward. They should offer valuable content in themselves but also have an offer for the product, service or training course as part of the event.

If you have an audience, you can work with others to present the webinar and pitch, and you can also offer links to evergreen webinars which people attend in their own time.

As an example, check out a replay of my webinar with Nick Stephenson, where we go into how to automate your author marketing at TheCreativePenn.com/nickjo

Questions:

- What are the pros and cons of affiliate income?

- How can you be an ethical and successful affiliate?

- How could you start making affiliate income?

- How will you expand this to increase traffic and revenue?

Resources:

- Smart Passive Income Guide to Ethical Affiliate Marketing — SmartPassiveIncome.com/guide/affiliate-marketing-strategies

- Amazon Associates — affiliate-program.amazon.com

- Apple's affiliate program — affiliate.itunes.apple.com/resources

- Rakuten affiliate for Kobo — rakutenadvertising.com/en-uk/affiliate

- Bookshop.org affiliate program — www.bookshop.org/affiliates/profile/introduction

- Sites for creating multi-links — Booklinker.net and Books2Read.com

- Pretty Links for WordPress to create easy to manage affiliate links — PrettyLinks.com

- My Tools page — www.TheCreativePenn.com/tools

2.3 Crowdfunding, patronage and subscription

"1,000 true fans is an alternative path to success other than stardom. Instead of trying to reach the narrow and unlikely peaks of platinum bestseller hits, blockbusters, and celebrity status, you can aim for direct connection with a thousand true fans."

Kevin Kelly, *1000 True Fans*

The most common way for writers to make a living is to create something first and then be paid for the product *after* it is produced by using the various publishing and media opportunities available. But the emergence and popularity of patron-funded creation and crowdfunding has provided creators with new ways to earn money.

You can get paid *before* you even create the work, and if you retain the rights, you can turn those products into other streams of income later. You can also earn recurring monthly payments that essentially provide a predictable 'salary' for your creative work.

This is all possible because a certain percentage of your fans love your work enough to pay upfront for a project or to support you monthly. They understand that the major online sites and big publishers leave little income for the creator, so this is a way to give back and receive extra limited-edition bonuses in return.

This type of income is most suitable for writers who already have an audience and have some way to reach them, as you need to drive supporters to the project. You also need to make sure you set aside the time to create whatever you promise for your one-off or monthly project.

Crowdfunding

Crowdfunding is designed for specific creative projects where many individual backers contribute a small sum of money upfront. If the project is funded, then the creator goes ahead with the project. Successful projects are also evidence of an engaged audience, and some authors have attracted book deals off the back of their Kickstarters.

In November 2020, multi-award-winning fantasy author Brandon Sanderson raised nearly US$7 million on Kickstarter to create the 10th anniversary leather-bound edition of *The Way of Kings*. Nearly 30,000 people supported his project for varying levels of pledge. Sanderson worked with a printer as well as professional artists to fulfill the project.

This is a great example of multiple streams of income, as Sanderson licensed other formats to traditional publishing but kept his special editions for his own projects.

Of course, Brandon Sanderson has a huge audience and most creators cannot fund such a big project, but start small and see what happens. Browse Kickstarter.com/publishing to find examples of projects currently underway for books and journalism.

If you want to crowdfund a project, do your research around best practices. There are horror stories of people under-budgeting and ending up out of pocket, so make sure you add a buffer for your time and cost out your pledge rewards and the final product in detail.

Dean Wesley Smith and Kristine Kathryn Rusch do regular Kickstarter projects to fund books, magazines, and anthologies. They also have a free course on Kickstarter best practices.

Patronage

Patron support is an ongoing revenue stream based on fans and supporters paying monthly, or for specific output in a form of membership.

Patreon.com is a popular patronage site used for all kinds of writing projects. Examples include:

Multi-award-winning and bestselling author Kristine Kathryn Rusch creates non-fiction articles about writing, publishing and creative business. Patrons receive her articles early and then Kris posts them on her blog at KrisWrites.com and also turns them into non-fiction books. Patreon.com/kristinekathrynrusch

Prolific, seven-figure independent author Lindsay Buroker creates fantasy and science fiction novels, releasing her new books to patrons first before publishing on Amazon and later on other stores. Patreon.com/lindsayburoker

Literary fiction, poetry and non-fiction author Orna Ross creates fiction and poetry at Patreon.com/OrnaRoss as well as providing help on how to self-publish poetry and plan creative projects.

It's not just for independent authors

Hugo and Nebula Award-Winning fantasy author Seanan McGuire creates short stories and poetry for her fans, some of which she later licenses into short story anthologies. Her novels are traditionally published under her own name as well as Mira Grant. Patreon.com/seananmcguire

It's not just for writing projects

Well-Read Black Girl is a writing community for Black and POC (Person of Color) writers at:

Patreon.com/wellreadblackgirl

Many authors use Patreon to support their podcasts

Thanks to my patrons for supporting The Creative Penn Podcast at Patreon.com/thecreativepenn where patrons receive an extra monthly Q&A audio and other benefits.

Mark Leslie Lefebvre uses Patreon for his Stark Reflections on Writing and Publishing show at Patreon.com/starkreflections and J. Thorn, J.D. Barker, and Zach Bohannon use it at Patreon.com/writersinkpodcast, among others.

Subscription email newsletters

Paid email newsletters are another possibility for subscription or membership. Writers of all genres spend a lot of time researching various topics, so we are often good at curation, as well as creation.

An email list is one of the most important business assets for authors, but usually this is a way to stay in touch with readers and fans and is free to sign up for. Paid email subscriptions are becoming more popular as a way to find the signal in the noise.

As an example, I subscribe to The Hotsheet, a paid bi-monthly newsletter on publishing by author and industry expert Jane Friedman.

Urban fantasy and non-fiction author T. Thorn Coyle uses Substack, which enables writers to offer paid email subscriptions, as well as video and audio.

She says, "Not only is Substack helping me connect to people more clearly, some people are happy to pay for my weekly newsletter even though they can get the same content for free. It's a deepening of my content marketing practice which I'm simply starting to call 'connecting to people.' My old newsletter just didn't work the same way for me, on any level. It felt like a chore, and I got very little engagement. Substack is easily shareable on social media and I get more engagement than I ever have before, plus income."

Platforms for subscription, membership, and tips

There are other platforms that enable this kind of ongoing monthly patron support, or one-off tips.

- Facebook offers Fan Subscriptions for Pages

- YouTube offers Channel Memberships

- Ko-fi.com and BuyMeACoffee.com ask fans to support your work for a tip or the price of a coffee

- ConvertKit Commerce offers recurring subscriptions for paid newsletters as well as one-off sales of digital products

More platforms are emerging all the time to help creators make a living from fans, so research what might work for you and your audience.

Questions:

- What are the benefits of crowdfunding?

- Research the publishing and writing section of Kickstarter and Indiegogo to find ideas for what you could create. What sparks your curiosity?

- What are the benefits of patronage or ongoing subscription?

- Research the writing and creative section of Patreon to find examples of creators who make a monthly income. What might work for your community?

- How could you successfully incorporate crowdfunding and/or patronage into your streams of income? What do you need to have in place to make this happen?

Resources:

- Kickstarter Creator Handbook — kickstarter.com/help/handbook

- Kickstarter Publishing and Journalism projects — Kickstarter.com/publishing

- Kickstarter projects by Dean Wesley Smith and Kristine Kathryn Rusch — www.kickstarter.com/profile/403649867/created

- Brandon Sanderson Way of Kings Kickstarter project — Kickstarter.com/projects/dragonsteel/the-way-of-kings-10th-anniversary-leatherbound-edition

- Kickstarter best practices course from WMG Publishing — wmg-publishing-workshops-and-lectures.teachable.com/p/kickstarter

- Patreon Creator Help — support.patreon.com

- YouTube Creator Academy — Creatoracademy.youtube.com/page/course/channel-memberships

- Facebook Fan Subscriptions — Facebook.com/creators/getting-started-with-fan-subscriptions

- The Hotsheet publishing email from Jane Friedman — hotsheetpub.com

- Substack for paid email newsletters — Substack.com

- Fan-supported tips — Ko-fi.com and BuyMeACoffee.com

- ConvertKit Commerce for recurring subscriptions — TheCreativePenn.com/convert

2.4 Professional speaking, teaching, performing, and live events

Speaking, teaching, performing and writing work well together because they offer different ways to deliver the same core message. They enable multiple streams of income through book sales and up-sell offers, as well as income from speaking fees and ticket sales.

Online speaking, teaching and performing is now more accessible than ever due to technological adoption in the pandemic, with top rates available for conferences and events that are now (at least partially) online.

Successful authors will need to speak at some point, whether that's at a conference, an online event, or in the media, so it's a skill that is well worth developing.

This section is just an introduction and if you're interested in pursuing this further, check out my book, *Public Speaking for Authors, Creatives and Other Introverts* on the practicalities, mindset, and business side of professional speaking.

Why 'professional' speaking?

Many writers speak and teach at conferences or online summits, or perform their work or read at library and bookstore events. However, many do this 'in return for' publicity or book sales, or other opportunities that may or may not follow.

Some publishers or events cover costs for authors, but often, it is at the writer's expense. This may leave the writer out of pocket if they have to travel somewhere and stay locally for the event so should be considered marketing rather than professional speaking, which is always paid.

I started speaking professionally back in 2008 when I published my first non-fiction book. I joined the National Speakers Association in Australia, where I lived at the time, and started to run my own events as well as delivering workshops and keynotes at conferences.

Over the years, I've spoken professionally in the US, UK, Europe and Asia Pacific, earning speaking fees and enjoying expenses-paid travel.

These days, speaking remains part of my author business, but I focus on topics I'm passionate about, events in locations I want to visit, or conferences that I'd like to attend anyway. I charge premium professional rates, and speaking opportunities come to me through my books, website, and podcast. If you regularly produce quality content that educates, inspires, or entertains, you are likely to be asked to speak at some point.

If you're unsure on speaker fees, check out the Society of Authors (UK) guidance on rates and fees. You can always translate that to your local currency and use it as a place to start.

Here are some of my top tips on speaking.

Decide on your target audience

The most highly paid professional speakers write nonfiction because their target market includes corporate events and conferences that have a significant budget. Fiction authors don't usually get paid much to speak at writing events (unless they are very famous) because the organizations that run them rarely have a lot of money to spend.

If you want to make five figures or more for a speaking event, then research the audience that will pay that kind of money before you choose your speaking topic, or even write your book.

Of course, you might have a passion that emerges from your writing — as I do! — which leads you to events that will never pay top dollar. That's okay, as long as you realize upfront the range of income opportunities available and adjust your expectations accordingly. Clearly, an inspirational keynote on leadership to a thousand people at a corporate conference will pay more than talking to a writers' group on self-publishing, or a school assembly, even though the latter options might be rewarding in other ways.

You have to choose your direction.

Decide on your speaking topic/s

If you have a book already, the topic will naturally suggest itself, and then you can consider the possibilities in detail. You can also decide on your target market and then design a talk or write a book that will appeal to them specifically.

Once you have your key topics, you can adjust your presentation per audience. Although I often speak on the same broad themes, no live presentation is the same, as I always update and tweak the content to make it specific to the audience.

Call yourself a speaker

Create a speaking page on your author website and add 'Speaker' to your business card. Include the topic/s you speak on, contact details, testimonials, and upcoming events.

As an example, my speaker page is at:

TheCreativePenn.com/speaking

Start speaking for free to gain experience as well as testimonials

If you're just getting started, speaking for free will help you build up experience, but start charging as soon as you can in order to make it a viable stream of income.

My first speaking event in 2008 was at a small writers' group in Brisbane, Australia, where I shared my story of self-publishing for the first time. I was nervous and sweaty, unsure of myself, and I'd spent many days preparing for what was a short talk for no money. But it was a start, and I asked for testimonials afterward to add to my brand new speaker page.

More than a decade later, I've spoken at conferences to thousands of people in theaters and conference centers, as well as to smaller audiences all over the world. You just have to get started and over time, you'll improve and so will your speaking income.

Understand and manage your anxiety

All speakers experience nerves or anxiety at some point, whether that's because of the number of people, the venue, or the importance of the opportunity. The trick is to reframe those feelings as positive energy that can take your performance to a new level and also see it as evidence that you are pushing your comfort zone and that you care about what you're doing. These are all good things!

I still go to the bathroom three times before going on stage — or even presenting on Zoom! My heart thumps and my mouth gets dry, but once I start speaking, those feelings dissipate. The key is to remember that it is never about you, it's all about the audience. Serve them and deliver great value for their time and money, and things will go well.

Up-skill and join a professional organization

Toastmasters is great for learning the basics, but if you want to be a paid professional speaker, then check out the National Speakers Association in America, the PSA in the UK or one of the other affiliated organizations from the Global Speakers Federation. You will learn practical and business skills as well as the confidence to charge what you're worth.

Questions:

- What are some benefits of speaking and how could you incorporate it as a stream of income?

- Research speakers in your niche. What can you learn from their websites around branding, pitching, products, and pricing?

- Who is your target market for professional speaking? How could you reach them? What rates do they pay?

- What topic/s could you speak on? Does this fit with your target market and your expectation of income?

- Do you need training and/or experience in order to charge for professional speaking? How will you develop these further?

Resources:

- *Public Speaking for Authors, Creatives and Other Introverts* — Joanna Penn

- The Society of Authors (UK) guidance on rates and fees: Societyofauthors.org/advice/rates-fees

- My speaking page — www.TheCreativePenn.com/speaking

- Toastmasters — www.toastmasters.org

- National Speakers Association USA — www.nsaspeaker.org

- Professional Speaking Association UK — www.thepsa.co.uk

- Global Speakers Federation with links to other country-specific sites — www.GlobalSpeakersFederation.net

2.5 Online courses, webinars, events, and membership sites

Many authors teach — either in colleges, universities and schools, or as part of writing courses, literary festivals, summits, and seminars.

Online training courses have grown in popularity over the last few years, but they have moved into the mainstream since the pandemic sent the world online. As an example, check out Masterclass, where famous writers teach writing, screenwriting, storytelling, and much more.

You can turn a live event or course into an online version or create a new digital product, and the available tools make it easier than ever. Once you know how to use basic video and audio software, you can also use those skills for book marketing. In an increasingly digital world, your ability to use these tools can help to set you apart and increase your income streams.

I've been creating and selling my own online courses for over a decade, as well as being an affiliate for others. You can find them at TheCreativePenn.com/courses

Why create an online course?

Perhaps you already teach in-person events and want to take them online, or you want to share your knowledge with students around the world and help others with your expertise.

You might want to increase your revenue with a higher value scalable product based on your book, as people pay more for multimedia material. You can also offer higher-priced extras like one-on-one support or a mastermind as up-sell options.

Decide on the type of course

There are many kinds of online training experiences now. Options include:

Live webinar series or event with replays for download: This model is used by many conferences that were previously only live events. Speakers deliver material live and the recordings are available later for replay. You can do this on a smaller scale by offering a webinar series or even an individual lecture with replay.

Evergreen online course: This is my preferred model, as you can set up the course and then it continues to sell over time. Students can buy the course anytime and work through the material at their own pace, starting as soon as they purchase. There is no overhead in terms of management or extra time. You can create courses of different lengths for different price points and even offer free options so people can try out your style of teaching.

Online course with scheduled start date and personal support and/or extras: This is the launch model approach where you open and close the course at various points during the year. This allows you to welcome a new cohort of students each time, supporting them at a prescribed pace with personal help and support or live events during the period of the course. These are usually priced higher than the other options, as you will need to spend more time with students.

Each of these options has benefits and drawbacks and there are many variations of each. Investigate courses in your niche and attend or purchase some so you can decide what might work for your audience and your lifestyle.

Decide on the topic

If you have a book (or a blog or a podcast) already, you could present that material in an alternative way to serve the needs of your existing audience.

You can also survey your audience and ask for their biggest questions around your area of expertise. This will give you a lot of material you can use within the course. I use Google Forms or you can use SurveyMonkey or equivalent tools.

Research what people are looking for in specific niches. Examine the bestselling books on Amazon in your sub-category, or check the top websites in your niche. Look at the top questions on Quora and/or questions on Twitter around a topic or join Facebook or LinkedIn groups on an area.

In order to be profitable, your course needs to be specific and address a painful problem that people will pay money to solve.

Plan the content and prepare your material

Start by brainstorming possibilities. If you have a book already, use your table of contents as a starting point. If you're a speaker, you might have presentation decks to work from. I often plan in Scrivener or in Keynote and create a skeleton of the major sections.

Expand this list into smaller bite-size chunks that you can turn into separate videos. A training course is a journey as much as reading a book should be, so organize it in a logical sequence that guides the customer through.

Use multimedia. You will create core videos and audio, but you could also consider PDF downloads, worksheets, workbooks, exercises, and other aspects that bring the material alive. You could create bonus videos with experts in a niche, as well as live webinars with participants and even curate a community on Facebook or another site. Some courses include homework and other one-on-one help, but this adds a lot of ongoing work and takes time, so be clear on the commitment you're willing to make.

Decide on your price point early on because this will guide how extensive the course should be. Don't spend months creating a mega course which will cost you time and money and perhaps only sell to a few people. Start with something small, especially with your first endeavor, as you will learn along the way and you can scale up over time.

Create a sales page that includes benefits to the customer, testimonials, and information about the content, as well as how to buy and Frequently Asked Questions. You're welcome to model any of mine at:

www.TheCreativePenn.com/courses

By the end of this preparation phase, I will have completed Keynote decks for each of my videos as well as the logos and images needed throughout. Everything is in place for recording.

Learn how to use the (basic) tools

You will need to use some technology in order to create your course and you will improve with practice. There is a learning curve for any new skill, but good news: it's a lot easier than it used to be!

Start with whatever you already have, for example, most laptops come with some form of basic video and audio software, or you can use your phone if necessary. Don't over-invest until you're sure what you need.

There are many options so investigate what might work for you. Currently, my technical setup is as follows:

- Blue Yeti USB microphone for high-quality audio

- Screenflow on Mac for video recording and screen capture as well as editing (or use Camtasia for PC)

- Zoom.us for recording interviews. It can also be used for webinars.

- Amadeus Pro for editing audio (or you can use free software Audacity)

- Keynote for slides (or use PowerPoint on PC)

I use Teachable for hosting, selling and managing the course, which means I don't have to maintain a separate site with plugins and a payment system.

I've done my own tech setup before and it is a huge pain, whereas with Teachable you pay a scalable monthly amount and they do all the maintenance. You basically drag and drop your finished files. They can also handle digital taxes for you. Super simple!

Record, edit, and publish your content

Once you have prepared your material, you need to record and edit it, then upload it to the site you use to publish.

Plan specific blocks of recording time. Creating video is like a performance, in that you have to project energy into your presentation. It can be tiring for introverts, so I set aside time in the morning for recording video or audio when I have the energy.

Plan longer than you need. If you have material for 30 minutes of video, then plan at least 90 minutes to record it. You will stop and start as you go through and you may find things you want to add. I find it easier to record several videos with all the mistakes and then go back later to edit them. Recording and editing will take always longer than you expect at the beginning.

Keep everything organized and backed up. I use separate folders for slides, raw video, edited video, audio, exercises, bonus interviews, etc. Make sure you also back up the material just in case. I use Dropbox and an external hard drive.

Open the doors!

Tell your audience about the course. If you have a website, podcast, or email list, then start by telling those who know you.

Go wider. All the usual principles of marketing apply when you sell a course, just as when you're selling a book. You can do content marketing—blog posts, podcast interviews, social media sharing, and you can also use paid advertising like Facebook Ads to attract your target market.

Work with affiliates. If you have a network of professionals within your niche, you can work with them to cross-promote your course with an affiliate link. Many of the platforms, including Teachable, offer a simple way to set up and manage affiliates.

All the online course hosting services, including Teachable, have training, webinars and help on how to optimize every stage of your course.

For more detail on my step-by-step process, check out my course on how to Turn What You Know Into An Online Course at:

www.TheCreativePenn.com/learn

Questions:

- What are the benefits of creating an online course? How could it form part of your multiple streams of income?

- What type of course might be useful to your audience?

- What topic will your course be on?

- How much time do you need to set aside for learning new skills, preparing and recording your course?

- What tools and technology do you need to investigate? What skills do you need to learn, and how could they be useful for your wider author business?

- What is stopping you from creating an online course?

Resources:

- Teachable for creating and selling online courses — TheCreativePenn.com/teachable

- My courses including on how to Turn What You Know Into An Online Course — www.TheCreativePenn.com/learn

- Masterclass courses by famous authors, writers, screenwriters and more — TheCreativePenn.com/masterclass

2.6 Advertising and sponsorship

If you have a significant audience, companies will want to advertise on your site or sponsor your podcast or video channel.

Whereas affiliate marketing means you are paid *after* a customer has clicked and bought the product or service, advertising and sponsorship involve upfront payment for promotion.

The same ethical principle applies, in that you should only work with companies that are useful to your audience and offer a great product or service. This is also important for retention of advertisers over time, because they need a return on their investment.

This stream of income has significantly increased for creators over the last few years, as video content and podcasting, in particular, have become more popular and companies want to pay for placement.

Advertising

Advertising options include an advert on your website, a link in your newsletter, a paid promotional article, or an ad in a video or podcast.

You can work with companies directly or choose passive advertising options where a company serves ads over or within your content.

Examples include YouTube advertising which I have on my channel at YouTube.com/thecreativepenn for some videos, or a company like Midroll.com for podcast advertising.

Successful author examples include steampunk author Meg La Torre at iWriterly, and Jenna Moreci, who both combine book sales with YouTube advertising and other streams of income.

Sponsorship

Ongoing sponsorship from a company implies a longer term relationship than one-off advertising and is often developed over time based on relationships in your niche.

My Creative Penn Podcast is sponsored by Kobo Writing Life, Draft2Digital, Findaway Voices, Ingram Spark, and ProWritingAid, companies I use personally and happily recommend. They have all continued to renew their podcast sponsorship because my audience is a good fit and they continue to receive a return on investment from appearing on the show.

If you want to earn money with advertising and sponsorship:

Develop a niche audience and have an effective way to reach them

This might be a website or blog, YouTube channel, podcast, or even a Facebook Page, Instagram channel or other social media platform.

Advertisers and sponsors need evidence of views, downloads, or clicks before they invest and as part of renewal negotiation. Prepare your numbers and create a Power-Point/Keynote deck or PDF with all the relevant details.

Decide on your rates

Your advertising rate will be based on the size of your measurable audience, placement type, how long the sponsorship is for — and your own confidence at asking. There are various industry rates listed online which you can use for starters. Increase your rates as your audience grows and don't lock in sponsors for too long, so you can raise your rates over time.

Keep creating content that your audience love

Ongoing advertising and sponsorship revenue is dependent on creating content that people consume and engage with, so you need to create for the long term to make it effective.

Your advertisers and sponsors are also your customers, so create content that resonates with their message. I try to match my sponsors with the episode topic, for example, ProWritingAid with an interview on editing and Findaway Voices with audiobooks.

Questions:

- Do you have a niche audience that is large enough to consider offering advertising or sponsorship?

- Which companies or services might work best for your audience?

Resources:

- Interview with Meg La Torre on her multiple streams of income based on her iWriterly YouTube channel: TheCreativePenn.com/youtubeincome

- My YouTube channel — www.YouTube.com/thecreativepenn

- iWriterly YouTube channel — www.youtube.com/iwriterly

- Jenna Moreci's YouTube channel — www.youtube.com/jennamoreci

2.7 Physical products and merchandise

"If someone likes the story you're telling,
likes it enough to become a fan of it, that person doesn't
just want another book, they also want related products
like t-shirts and mugs and stuffed animals, and pretty
much anything you can think of."

Kristine Kathryn Rusch, *Rethinking The Writing Business*

If you want to run a global, scalable business from a laptop
(as I do), it's much easier to focus on digital products and
online services. Physical products are more expensive to
create and they require design, manufacturing, storage and
shipping. They are difficult to update if there are problems,
and it's much harder to manage refunds.

But people love physical products, and we all buy a lot of
them!

They also offer the potential to accelerate brand recogni-
tion, bring in other streams of income, and can also be
used for marketing.

Of course, we're not all going to have our characters on
everything from lunchboxes to games and theme park
rides like Harry Potter, but if you consider that many
independent musicians make more from merchandise
than they do from music sales and streaming, it's worth
investigating as another stream of income, especially if you
enjoy the more visual aspect of the publishing industry.

While product sales and merchandising could expand
your reach, they should also make you money. If you

attend conventions or conferences, you'll find tables full of 'swag,' bookmarks, notebooks, pens, branded sweets, and postcards. These are for marketing purposes only and they are an expense, not an income stream, so are not considered here.

Options for products and merchandise

The kind of products and/or merchandise you create will depend on your audience, your books, your brand, your business goals — and your imagination!

For non-fiction, you could use your logo, tagline or quotes. For example, I have mugs, bags, stickers and stationery at Society6.com/creativepenn with the word 'creative' and the affirmation "I am creative. I am an author," which I had in my wallet for years before I published my first book.

Author and illustrator, Randall Munroe at XKCD.com offers t-shirts and posters of his art, as well as stickers, mugs, and buttons.

Romance author J.A. Huss includes everything from t-shirts and hoodies, to tote bags, furniture and wall art, phone covers and even a yoga mat featuring her romance cover art and branding from her various series at Society6. com/jahuss

Plush toys are a good option for children's authors. Wendy H. Jones writes across multiple genres and her children's book, *Bertie the Buffalo,* has a matching soft toy of the cute main character.

Peter Ball from Brain Jar Press says, "Writers produce a lot of content by virtue of being writers, and there's very little thought put into making money out of the bulk of that content. Even something as simple as a particularly pithy tweet that earned a lot of likes might have a second life as a limited run of stickers/keychains/coffee mugs/etc if you've got an audience looking for engagement."

For more ideas, check out *Merchandise for Authors* by Melissa Addey, which features ideas from authors across multiple genres.

Print-on-demand

While it's common to use print-on-demand services for books, there are also options for merchandise. Just upload high-resolution images and apply them to various products.

Popular sites include Redbubble, Teespring, Zazzle, and Society6, which offer multiple product types. There are also more specialist sites like Spoonflower for fabric designs. More sites emerge all the time, so do your research and make sure you test the products, as quality may vary.

Custom-made products

Fantasy author Kimberley Ward makes custom jewelry, miniature terrariums, and small sculptures which she sells alongside her books on Etsy at WardsWhimsicalWorks.

She says, "I don't view it exclusively as merchandise, it's my escape. I love sculpting and making quirky jewelry. It's a way that I can remain attached to my growing stories even when I'm not actively writing, and it keeps the imagination flowing. The fact that I can make it tie in with my fantasy novels is an extra win and people can buy and enjoy the products without having to read the books beforehand, plus they can support me and my business through different avenues.

It's not easy, as it can take a lot of time and energy to maintain, so you need to be dedicated and have a passion for creating."

Bigger projects and licensing your brand

If you have a significant audience and an idea that they might love, you could use crowdfunding platforms like Kickstarter to raise money for custom design and production. Browse the various categories of Games, Art, Publishing, and more for ideas.

You can also consider licensing your brand to manufacturing and distribution companies to create new products. Traditional publishers do this with their brands, and independent authors are expanding into this area too.

For more detail, read *Rethinking The Writing Business* by Kristine Kathryn Rusch.

Beware of over-enthusiasm!

It can be tempting to dive into the world of print-on-demand merchandising, coming up with all kinds of exciting things to sell. But, as with our books, sales depend on marketing.

You will not sell any merchandise if you don't promote it, so you could create all kinds of things on the print-on-demand sites with nothing to show for your time. If you go ahead with custom product creation, you could also spend too much money and end up out of pocket.

Start small with something you think your audience might buy and use a print-on-demand service to test the market. Only expand into more developed ideas once you have some experience and have done extensive research.

Science fiction and fantasy author Joseph Lallo created fantasy coins and mascot figurines for his fans and has advice for authors who want to create merchandise.

"The high-risk, high-reward option is to produce something distinctive that your readers will connect with and haven't seen before. Print-On-Demand figurines are possible from places like Shapeways. They have the same pros and cons as print-on-demand t-shirts, but are much more novel and interesting. You'll likely be paying a digital sculptor a few hundred dollars to produce the file for these.

I commissioned a run of custom metal coins for a fantasy book release from Campaign Coins. They cost less than a dollar to produce and were an easy sell at $5 each, all while weighing just a few ounces and thus cheap to ship. These options almost always have a significant upfront cost, but making them a limited run event and funding them as their own Kickstarter or as a stretch goal to a broader Kickstarter can eliminate these costs and also allow you to precisely predict demand.

Be fully aware of the production challenges before doing this, however. Set expectations for an extended lead-time before production to avoid disappointing or frustrating fans."

A caution on image use

However you publish, it's unlikely that you have the right to use your book cover art on merchandise, unless it is specifically listed in your contract with your publisher or your designer.

Most book cover designers use stock art and license images for use on book covers only. Check your contracts before going ahead with any ideas, or commission exclusive art for specific merchandise.

Questions:

- What are the pros and cons of physical products and merchandising? How do these differ from swag?

- What aspects of your books or business might be relevant for products and merchandising?

- What could you create through print-on-demand? What might need to be a bigger project with more funding?

- Do you have the right to use the images related to your books on merchandise?

Resources:

- *Merchandise for Authors: Engage Your Readers While Increasing Your Income* — Melissa Addey

- *Rethinking The Writing Business* — Kristine Kathryn Rusch

- Print-on-demand merchandise sites — Redbubble.com, Teespring.com, Zazzle.com, and Society6.com

2.8 Freelance writing and ghostwriting

Freelance writing is writing for hire. This can range from writing articles for online or print media; copywriting, technical and specialist writing; gaming or other media; writing for licensed brands and spin-off shows; and any other forms of writing where you're paid for your words or your time and you don't own the final product.

Ghostwriting is writing books which are published under your client's name, and while ghostwriters are usually contractually bound to keep their clients secret, it is a common practice in the publishing industry. The rates can be significant if you develop a track record of writing fast in the client's voice.

For both of these areas, you're paid per project or by word count and usually, you don't own the rights to the finished product. Check your contract for specific terms.

Choose projects carefully

Research the best-paying markets and clients, learn from successful freelancers who are making a living, and specifically target higher-paying opportunities. If you end up writing for content mills at tiny rates, you will burn out and hate writing. Only apply for freelance jobs that fit your ideal situation.

Differentiate yourself and demonstrate that you're worth the investment for higher rates. If you're just starting out, you may well have to work for free to get those first credits under your belt, but don't let that period stretch out for too long.

Work smarter, not harder

Writing on more difficult and in-depth topics will earn you more money and set you apart, so consider where your expertise lies and go deep within a niche. Develop and foster relationships with key clients so work comes to you, instead of having to chase it all the time.

Network with other freelance writers so you become part of a community and refer work to other people if appropriate. Over time, others will refer you in turn and your freelance work will become more of an ecosystem.

Use the various tools available to help write faster and smarter, for example, use editing tools like ProWritingAid or Grammarly, as well as time management and invoicing tools so you keep track of submissions and payments.

Showcase your writing on your website

When I hire freelance writers for content articles, I always check their website first. I want to see examples of their writing and also find out more about them so I can see if we might be a good fit.

Create a professional site that includes a personal About page and information on projects you specialize in, as well as examples of your writing.

Balance money for time with building assets for long-term income

Freelancing and ghostwriting are money for time. You can only earn income once from your words.

Make sure that you balance writing for others with writing for yourself. Set aside time to build your intellectual property assets, write your own books, and maintain your brand so that you can earn more money in the future from scalable means.

Equestrian writer Elizabeth McCowan says, "My main source of income is content and ghostwriting for other people, but I always schedule time in my day to write on my own projects. I treat myself as one of my clients. This thought process gives me the authority to pursue my own writing in a positive and forward-thinking way. Just like I do with all my paying customers."

Tips from a professional freelance travel writer

Sarah Baxter is an award-winning freelance travel writer with over a decade of experience writing for publications such as Wanderlust, Lonely Planet, and The Telegraph, as well as the author of travel books including *A History of the World in 500 Walks*. Here are her tips for making a living as a freelance writer.

Rule 1: Don't write for free or for 'exposure'

You can't make a living with your writing if it's not paying you anything—that's not a job, it's a hobby. Be serious about pursuing this as a career. Also, if you write for a pittance, you make it tougher for every other freelancer to get paid a decent fee.

Think broad

While a cover feature in the New York Times might be the dream, it's unlikely to be the first writing gig you get. It's perfectly valid to aim high, but what else is out there?

Look small and local. Look niche. Look at websites and newsletters. Look at the publications of businesses and organizations. Mix it up.

Most successful freelance writers will write a wide variety of content for an array of outlets. They will write lovely flowing pieces for national newspapers but also a column for a specialist magazine, commercial web content for company X, a newsletter for organization Y, a book for publisher Z...

Some of it will be thrilling, some of it will be bread-and-butter stuff. But it all adds up to a living and keeps things interesting. And you never know when a small piece for an out-there magazine might lead to something bigger or better.

Thinking broad can also increase the value of one idea

For instance, a commission for an article paying, say, a £400 fee, is no good if researching and writing the piece is going to take you two weeks. That's less than £30 a day. Less than UK minimum wage.

You could (and likely should) request a higher fee. But you can also look to get multiple pieces out of the same period of research so you effectively earn more in the same amount of time. It also forces you to flex your creative muscles: how can you spin that original idea in multiple ways, to create different stories for different publications?

If you have always wanted to write for a particular outlet, approach it seriously

Read past issues of that publication, look at the stories it has published in the past, get a feel for its style. Read its contributor guidelines. Find out the email address of the right person to pitch to for the right section. Follow its editors and/or staff writers on social media.

Look at who is writing the pieces – if all the interviews are bylined to in-house writers, it's probably not worth pitching those, but if the publication has a guest column or a regular feature type that's always by a freelancer, start there.

Build your skill set

You want to make money from your writing, but you might be more likely to get work if you can also provide quality photography, video content, related workshops, Instagram stories, or social media posts. Look at ways you might be able to add value to your offering and consider taking relevant courses.

Be nice

Not a push-over – you should be willing to ask for higher fees or turn down jobs that just aren't right. But always be nice about it. Building connections and nurturing relationships is key when you are your own business.

Editors talk to each other and move around. You might not care about insulting the editor of Koi Carp Weekly, because you never want to write for them again, but what about – five years later – when that person is features editor of National Geographic?

Questions:

- What are the pros and cons of freelance writing and/ or ghostwriting?

- How could you develop this stream of income for your author business?

Resources:

- 71 ways to make money as a freelance writer. Guide from The Write Life on paying freelance opportunities with specific rates, as well as the practical information, including how to pitch, land clients, set rates and create invoices —
www.TheCreativePenn.com/freelance

- TheWriteLife.com — Helping writers create, connect and earn with articles and resources for freelancers

- MakeALivingWriting.com — Six-figure freelancer Carol Tice has been helping freelance writers for almost a decade. The site provides resources, articles and books to help freelance writers make money.

2.9 Consulting or coaching

If you're an expert in a niche and you regularly produce content that educates, inspires or entertains, you will attract people who want to pay for your expertise.

One of the easiest ways to make income online is to offer your services and with the explosion of online video calling during the pandemic, people are now used to working over the internet. It's easier than ever to reach a global audience.

Add a page on your website with Hire me, Book me, or Work with me, include what you offer and a button to Buy Now. You can use PayPal or Stripe or even a service like Teachable which includes a Coaching option, to process payments.

Here are some tips for coaching and consulting services.

Be clear on what you offer and your ideal client

Your sales page should include details of how the session works and options for payment. Is this a one-off session or monthly calls for a minimum amount of time? How long will the session last? Is it recorded? Are there extra components? What is the rate?

You also want to make it clear who the service is for, as you only want to attract your ideal client.

Include testimonials

Work for free with a few initial clients and ask for testimonials from happy customers as social proof that you know what you're talking about. If you offer great value, you'll also get word-of-mouth referrals over time.

If you're overwhelmed with too much work, put your rates up

I started out consulting on self-publishing back in 2009 for US$99 per hour but the amount of work grew with my profile and the popularity of the industry, so I put my rates up until they reached US$250 per hour.

I no longer consult, preferring to focus on scalable income streams, but this principle of raising rates is a good way to manage your workload and value your time.

Use a questionnaire so the client can articulate what they want before the session

It's important to find out what your client wants, determine their expectations, and figure out how you can provide value. A questionnaire can help you to prepare the session so it works well for both parties.

Don't be afraid to turn down a client if they don't match your services. Recommend others in the niche who might serve them better instead.

Record the call for a value-added experience

You can use Zoom or Skype or other online platforms to conduct your coaching or consulting sessions. You can also record the call and send that to the client afterward with any extra notes.

Model successful coaches and consultants

Find people in your niche to model in terms of their sales page and customer experience. Don't be afraid to start small and grow over time.

Coaching can be specific by genre. Four bestselling UK crime writers offer coaching as well as editing services at CrimeFictionCoach.com.

It can also work in groups or as part of a Mastermind. Author and editor, J. Thorn, offers small group coaching as part of The Author Success Mastermind.

Creative coach Mark McGuinness only works with successful creatives and uses a series of questions to make it clear who his service is for at LateralAction.com/coaching.

While Mark makes most of his business income through coaching, books play a critical part. He says, "If you are a coach, speaker, or consultant, then the value of a book to your business extends way beyond the royalties you earn on sales. My books have brought me many coaching clients as well as other opportunities, such as speaking at international conferences and offers from big publishers.

The act of writing a book forces you to clarify your thinking and lay your ideas out in an engaging and useful way. So writing deepens your expertise, even as it demonstrates it.

The act of reading the book requires your reader to engage deeply with your ideas and spend time in your world. So it's a powerful way to establish credibility and build a connection with potential clients and collaborators.

The back matter is key to leveraging the book for your business: include a professional biography, details of your services and other books, and invitations to engage with your ideas on your website or other platforms. For example, my back matter includes my podcast and the free course available at my website."

Questions:

- What are the pros and cons of offering consulting or coaching services?

- What could you help people with?

- Who are the successful coaches and consultants in your niche? What can you learn from them and model in order to set up and grow your own service?

Resources

- Teachable Coaching platform:
  TheCreativePenn.com/teachable

2.10 Author services

Many writers have other useful skills and offer author services to supplement their income from books and other writing.

Editing, manuscript critique, and/or proofreading

Literary fiction and memoir author Roz Morris also writes non-fiction books, teaches writing courses for The Guardian, and offers in-depth developmental editing.

She says, "I've always worked with books and magazines and editing is as natural to me as breathing. It also happens to be a natural complement to writing, keeping my critical faculties tuned. Every editing job brings up its own problems, which then help me in my own work. And it's rewarding to take a piece that's rough in some way – whether it's a full-length manuscript or an article of a few pages – and buff it so that it's professionally ready.

In terms of my time, some months are more balanced than others, but it works out in the end. With editing and other services, you need to fit others' deadlines. You are part of someone else's process and you need to be flexible. I'm very organized about splitting everything into tasks with their own deadlines, and that's how I write my own books. I used to run 30 titles at a time when I ran an editorial department so I'm used to multitasking."

You can find options for editors, proofreaders, and more at TheCreativePenn.com/editors

Specialist reading

There are opportunities for paid reading, for example, if you're a specialist in a particular area, you can offer specific feedback on certain areas, for example, an ex-police officer with expertise for crime writers, or a volcanologist with knowledge of earthquakes and volcanoes, or a sensitivity reader for gender or sexuality issues.

Book cover design

Thriller and urban fantasy author A.D. Starrling also designs book covers at 17 Studio Book Design. She says, "Design has always been in my blood. Turning it into a business that complements my writing career and earns an additional income is just the icing on the cake."

You can find more options for book cover design at:

TheCreativePenn.com/bookcoverdesign

Formatting

Award-winning mystery and memoir author Alexandra Amor is also my wonderful virtual assistant and offers services for authors.

She says, "Formatting books, and also coaching authors through the publishing process if they need it, has provided me with two additional streams of income that are fun and creative. It feels great to be able to offer this support to new independent authors while also adding another source of income to my author business. I balance my time between all these activities by blocking time for each one. Writing fiction comes first every day when I'm freshest, and then I focus on the other income streams for the rest of the day."

You can find more formatting options at:

TheCreativePenn.com/formatting

Marketing

Many authors want help with marketing so if you love it and have demonstrated success, this can be a great service to offer.

Non-fiction author, project manager, and book launch strategist Courtney Kenney says, "Your income doesn't have to be entirely from books. Consider how your current skills and knowledge can be combined with writing. Maybe you offer something nobody else does. In my case, I knew I wanted to get out of my boring day job as a project manager for a company I didn't care about. I took on my first book launch client as a leap of faith, learning as I went.

Flash forward four years and my company of one is thriving and making six figures. Combining my experience in project management with my passion for books and publishing was the best decision I ever made. I created my own job. Think about the unique talents you possess and create your next job. What next step gives you more freedom to create?"

You can find free online courses and more people to help with your marketing at:

TheCreativePenn.com/reedsy

Research assistant

Ann Thomson writes speculative fiction as well as fantasy, poetry and non-fiction. She is also an anthropologist and works as a researcher-for-hire for various short-term assignments for the local university. She says,

"I find my research projects primarily through word of mouth and industry connections. Because I work primarily in anthropology, I am able to bring a tolerant approach to the cultures I use and those I create in my stories. I am able to play with the elements hiding inside folklore and mythology and do so with an awareness of the importance of these archetypes culturally. I like to think this has given me discipline and an eye for structure and the mechanics of writing, as well as awareness of how to write for different target audiences.

If you want to do research for hire, I advise making connections. I share articles I write with my peers and fellow researchers through academic groups and LinkedIn, and we share things we find important with each other."

Small press publishing

Some authors turn their passion and experience in publishing into running a small press to publish other authors.

Award-winning literary fiction, poet, and memoir author Jessica Bell set up Vine Leaves Press to "blur the line between commercial and experimental works." A multi-passionate creative, Jessica is also a singer/songwriter and graphic designer. She says, "If you want to start your own small press, be a patient and understanding person. If you're not, you will run into trouble and conflict with your authors.

Be ambitious and have the ability to look into the future regarding expectation. You will not make money straight away. During the first five years, we were just breaking even every year; sometimes we would even have a loss, and that was with volunteers on our team!

Eight years and over eighty books later, we are finally making a decent profit. I think that comes down to the fact that I didn't want to compromise on content. I refused to go mainstream. There are books out there, unique books, that need to be read.

To make it as a small press, I say, don't settle for the same-old. Be as innovative as you can. Post something on social media EVERY DAY. Build a mailing list. Approach publishing like a self-publisher. Traditional methods used by the Big 5 do not work for a small press. You will end up bankrupt. One of our biggest sellers is a vignette collection (The Walmart Book of the Dead). It sells because it really is unique and intriguing. Market to niche audiences, not the world."

Other possibilities

There are many other options for services that authors need at various stages, and if you have particular skills, one of them can be a valuable extra source of income.

A virtual assistant can help with publishing and marketing tasks, website management, email lists, book launches, and more.

If you have technical skills, then setup and maintenance of author websites is an option.

Audiobooks need editing and mastering, and podcasts need editing and production. If you have audio experience, or you're interested in learning, this is definitely an expanding area.

Translation is another option as more authors move into publication and sales in other languages.

If you want to offer services, then consider applying for Partner Membership of the Alliance of Independent Authors. Potential clients will know that you offer a good service and you'll be able to network with indie authors within the organization.

Warning: Services can eat your life!

While offering services for authors can be a great way to bring in immediate income, it can also take up all your time.

You might find it a challenge to attract work when you first start out, but as your reputation grows and the word spreads, you may find yourself inundated. Set boundaries for the time you spend with clients and carve out time to write and build your own scalable creative assets, as they will bring you income for the long term.

Questions:

- Do you want to offer services to authors? What would be the best fit for your skills, and what does the author community need?

- How will you balance your time between clients and your own creative work?

Resources:

- Alliance of Independent Authors for Partner Membership — www.AllianceIndependentAuthors.org/partnership-approval

- Reedsy marketplace for vetted professionals: www.TheCreativePenn.com/reedsy

- List of editors — www.TheCreativePenn.com/editors

- List of book cover designers — www.TheCreativePenn.com/bookcoverdesign

- List of formatters — www.TheCreativePenn.com/formatting

2.11 Other ways to make money with your writing

In January 2021, I did a survey on author streams of income as research for this Third Edition. While the most common income streams are covered in the previous sections, these are some other ways that writers make money with their words.

You can find a full breakdown of the survey results in Appendix 4.

Grants, endowments, fellowships, prizes, competitions, and other funding

In many countries, there are various funding opportunities available to writers through Arts Councils, author organizations and other government or privately funded options.

Award-winning historical fiction author Melissa Addey completed a creative writing PhD with full funding and runs a course at the British Library in London on applying for grants. She says,

"I've been fortunate to have secured £75,000 over five years in different grants, including my PhD. Many writers don't realize what support there is out there, but it's very much worth understanding the grants available from different sources and spending some time learning how to write a good bid. You won't always secure the funds, of course, as there is a lot of competition, but there is a spiral of success that happens.

Grant funders tend to look favorably on you the more grants you've received, if you can show a return on their investment: that you did something worthwhile and interesting with their money, which took your career to another level. Look out for the Society of Authors who regularly run a ticketed event showcasing available grants, as a good starting point, and if you want to undertake a creative writing PhD, make sure to ask the universities about the funding available."

Literary prizes and competitions can also bring in income, but of course, applying does not guarantee winning. Some have significant prize money, and many have submission fees. Some are valuable for publishing credit and marketing exposure, and others are a waste of time and not worth the entry fee. There are many lists of prizes and competitions, so evaluate your definition of success and what is worth applying for.

Public Lending Rights and Licensing and Collection Services

Some countries have agencies that provide payment for library lending. This includes Canada, UK, Ireland, Australia, New Zealand, Germany and many other European countries. Register your work and you'll receive payment automatically once or twice per year.

Horror and non-fiction author Mark Leslie Lefebvre says, "I've long been a fan of multiple streams of income for writers, and one of those important streams in this Canadian author's life is the annual Public Lending Right check. For the past several years, my annual PLR check has been larger than any single royalty statement from any of the publishers I work with. And every year it keeps growing. In fact, for the past several years, the check was enough to cover the cost of an all-inclusive week-long trip to the Dominican Republic.

A single match on one of my books in a Canadian library earns me about 25 times what I get from a single retail sale through my publisher. If you are an author in a country with a Public Lending Right program and you aren't registered for it, you're potentially leaving a significant amount of money on the table."

Magazines and periodicals — online or printed

Karen Lock Kolp produces a monthly We Turned Out Okay Playbook, a quality printed, subscription-only resource for parents teaching simple, powerful tools to help family life. She's also the author of several parenting books, a podcaster, speaker, and coach.

She says, "Really know your audience, and find ways to inject yourself into your writing. I include a mindfulness essay in the playbook, and although I was downright afraid to include something so personal at first, I knew my readers — parents of young children — needed that place of calm and peace. I tried it and it worked. It's routinely spoken of as a favorite part of the playbook."

Serial reading sites

Wattpad is the most widely known serial reading site, with 90 million active users worldwide. It's a social platform where authors post regularly and engage with readers directly.

Successful books have been turned into movies through Wattpad Studios or found traditional book deals through Wattpad Books. While primarily a marketing platform, you can link to your books on various stores, and they offer Paid Stories for select writers as direct monetization.

There are other serial reading sites including Radish, Tapas, Webnovel, and more, and each has its own genre focus and options for monetization. Serial writing is most suited to books with multiple arcs and cliffhangers to keep people reading.

Commissioned writing

Susan E. Farriss, author of Southern Gothic and poetry, also writes poetry on commission, creating a unique gift for a special occasion. After a discussion about the person or situation, she writes a one-of-a-kind poem. She also offers love letter assistance for Valentine's Day and anniversaries.

Work with other creatives to transform your words

Jack and Kitty Norton are Emmy Award-winning writers, audio artists, filmmakers, and musicians. Jack says, "My wife is a composer. She has taken my words (poems, lines and scraps from short stories) and turned them into songs. She records them and distributes them wide on all music platforms. We also publish the tunes and work with ASCAP. Songs like this have been used in movies, TV shows and commercial jingles and we get royalties from all those opportunities as well!"

Turn your writing profits into other assets that bring in more income

Consider taking a percentage of your profits and use it to diversify outside of the writing business entirely. Some writers invest in property, others in stocks or index funds, and others in separate businesses. Find what works for you based on your interests and country-specific tax and investment rules.

For more options and ideas, check out my recommended books and podcasts at TheCreativePenn.com/moneybooks

Questions:

* Do any of these additional ideas spark your curiosity? How could you take the next step?

Resources:

* The Society of Authors list of grants — SocietyOfAuthors.org/Grants

* FundsForWriters list of grants — FundsForWriters.com/grants

* Authors Guild list of contests, grants, and residences — AuthorsGuild.org/category/contests-grants

* Arts Council UK grants — Artscouncil.org.uk/projectgrants

* PLR for UK and Ireland — www.plr.uk.com

* ALCS for UK — www.alcs.co.uk

* PLR for Canada — PublicLendingRight.ca

* List of countries with PLR schemes — plrinternational.com/established

* Wattpad information for writers — www.wattpad.com/writers

- Alliance of Independent Authors list of awards and contests — www.SelfPublishingAdvice.org/author-awards-contests-rated-reviewed

- List of book and novel-writing competitions — www.christopherfielden.com/short-story-tips-and-writing-advice/book-and-novel-competitions.php

- List of short story competitions and awards — www.christopherfielden.com/short-story-tips-and-writing-advice/short-story-competitions.php

The transition to making a living with your writing

"We discover the possibilities by doing, by trying new activities, building new networks, finding new role models. We learn who we are in practice, not in theory."

David Epstein, *Range:*
Why Generalists Triumph in a Specialized World

This book has given you lots of options on how to make a living from your writing, and I hope you're inspired by the possibilities. But I don't recommend that you quit your job right away, because these options take time to build.

Here are some manageable steps for how you can transition to making a living from your writing, or build up more income streams on the side while maintaining your day job, as I did for the first five years of my writing career.

(1) Decide on your focus

Don't try to do everything at once!

Before you jump into the practical steps, spend some time considering your definition of success, what you want to create and how you want to make a living with your writing, as well as what might fit into your lifestyle.

The questions in each chapter might help you to figure out which direction to take. You can find a consolidated list in Appendix 3 and you can download them at:

TheCreativePenn.com/makealivingdownload

There's also a Companion Workbook available in print with all the questions so you can write in that if you prefer.

Follow your curiosity and enthusiasm. Which areas spark the most ideas?

Ignore the rest for now.

You also need to find what suits you as a creative personality. Some authors find great success focusing on only one thing, for example, writing and publishing in the same genre. If that satisfies you, it's a fantastic way to make a living with your writing — but it's not for everyone.

I'm a multi-passionate creator. My fiction is cross-genre and I love podcasting and audio as a way to express another aspect of my creativity. I enjoy helping writers with my non-fiction, and I love having multiple streams of income. It enables me to be independent and financially secure in a fast-changing world.

You need to choose your focus based on what you want to write and how you want to make a living.

Romance author Sally Rose says, "Decide what YOU love and really want to do, then stay focused and avoid shiny object syndrome.

It's so easy to get distracted by 'all the things' when reading what other authors are doing, especially when they're posting big success stories. It's caused me to second guess my plans (repeatedly) and skip around on lots of different ideas when I should have stayed focused on building momentum.

Lesson learned.

Now I keep my eyes on my own paper and I'm working toward my own goal which makes me much happier."

(2) Find people to model

When I decided to leave my job and become an author entrepreneur over a decade ago, I knew it was possible because I could see others who were living the way I wanted to. Those role models made it possible to believe that I could do it too, and I still have people I follow for that reason.

Find people who make an income doing what you want to do. Read their books and their blogs. Buy their courses. You might even be able to pay for consulting. You could also email them, but respect their time and only ask intelligent questions after you've been through all of their publicly available material.

You might find your role models across different parts of the industry, as I have. For example, writing craft from one author, blogging and podcasting from another, and book sales from someone else again. This is a great way to put together a way of creative business that really works for your situation.

Curate the voices you listen to with care along the way. Is their advice relevant for the direction you want to go?

For example, a traditionally published author who started out twenty years ago will have a different view of the publishing industry to an indie author making money online right now. An editor in a publishing house on a fixed salary can tell you what their imprint wants to publish, but they can't tell you how to make multiple streams of income from your intellectual property assets.

Your role models will change over time as you grow in experience and confidence, and perhaps you will even be a role model for others in the future.

(3) Stop overthinking. Take the first step.

If you want to make a living with your writing, then you need to put your words into the world. Whatever direction you choose, you can take the first step with something small, but you need to take it.

Think about skiing down a steep hill.

You don't go in a straight line from top to bottom — you would quickly crash and burn!

You zigzag down, and sometimes you won't feel like you're making any progress at all. But you'll speed up as you gain experience, and you'll soon be having fun on the advanced slopes. It just takes time and practice.

You also need to be moving in order to change direction, and that's a key principle for your writing too. Reading books and taking courses are worthwhile, but you will progress more quickly if you write words, work with professional editors, and play with the available tools.

One day of practical experience can propel you forward far more quickly than trying to learn without doing. Like skiing, you need to get out there and try it. Fall down, get up again, and improve with experience.

If you don't already make some income from your writing, then get started. Prepare something for sale and actually sell it. Making that first ten dollars is magical, because if you can make ten, you can make a hundred, or a thousand, and you can do that every month, or even every day.

Start with an ebook or a course or sell your services — anything to prove that you can make some income based on your writing. You will learn by doing and your confidence will grow.

Poker Strategy author Barry Carter advises, "Just start. Put something out there to begin with, learn from it, then make it better. I think the biggest barrier to success is people waiting for permission to publish something."

Award-winning writer, artist and creativity coach Kaecey McCormick says, "There is an old Chinese proverb: 'The best time to plant a tree was twenty years ago. The second best time is now.' Don't let fear of it being too late to the writing world stop you from starting!

I was afraid I was too old, too late to the game when I started writing professionally, but I did it anyway. I now make more money as a writer than most of my friends who work at traditional jobs.

My next goal is to shift the bulk of my income from freelance writing to income from my books. Sometimes the feeling that I'm too old or that it's too late comes creeping in, but then I remember the proverb and my previous successes and get back to writing!"

If you're struggling to get started, set a deadline for yourself and stick it somewhere you will see it every day. Only you can make this happen. How much do you want it?

(4) Expand your streams of income

If you're already making some money from your writing, then start expanding your possibilities.

Are you leaving money on the table?

For example, if you're traditionally published in UK/Commonwealth, you could self-publish in the US and other territories. Or, if you have non-fiction books, have you created paperback editions and workbooks? Or could you turn the material into an online course?

What other ideas spark your curiosity? How can you expand into those areas?

You can also increase your income by building your audience. More readers mean more book sales. More traffic to your website means more affiliate income and sales of books and courses. More engaged subscribers to your email list can result in more sales and an ability to sell direct and make higher profits. How could you improve your marketing to make the most of these opportunities?

Focus on one area, learn the tools and technology, then apply them to your creative business, one step at a time.

Rachael Herron, author of thrillers, romance, memoir and non-fiction, says, "Say yes to trying everything. You might be surprised at what you really love doing. Then, when you can afford to, say no to everything except what you love."

Fantasy and non-fiction author Travis Senzaki says, "Diversifying your income streams is great, but just like advertising, don't try to do everything at once. Get one income stream going first and when you're comfortable that you can maintain that, grow another.

For my non-fiction, I started with an advice blog with ads, then added ebooks, print books, then coaching in response to my audience's needs. My next steps to consider are workbooks, a podcast, and online courses, but I'm not going to take them on all at once! For my fiction, each book, format, and retailer is an income stream. I focus on getting the ebook done first, as the core format, then expand from there."

As you take each step on the journey, keep focusing on your definition of success.

Fantasy and romance author Clare Sager says, "Don't compare yourself to others. Only look at how you're performing now compared to your past self. You might not be making the same as that six-figure author who just posted in a Facebook group, but are your average monthly sales this year higher than they were last year? It might not be sexy, but it is progress."

(5) Find your tribe

I still remember how lonely I was in the early years of my writing journey. I was living in Brisbane, Australia, working as an IT consultant. I didn't know any other writers at first and when I eventually found some groups, people looked down on me for self-publishing.

I started podcasting to connect with authors, and then I found virtual friends on Twitter, many of whom are now my friends in real life. It took time, but now I'm part of a thriving community who understand the challenges of writing and creative business.

You need a community of writers who understand the challenges you will face. As much as your family and friends love you, they are not your ideal readers, and they won't understand the inevitable creative and marketing hurdles we all have to tackle.

You need help and support in the difficult times, and you will also be able to lend a hand to those coming after you. You need people who will support your choices and your definition of success.

There are many organizations for authors and writers, so research the ones that might work for you. I'm a Member of ITW (International Thriller Writers) as well as the Horror Writers Association as my genre-specific groups.

I'm an Advisor and active member of the Alliance of Independent Authors, an international organization for indie-minded creatives, and also a member of the Society of Authors in the UK. I'm part of the Wide for the Win Facebook group, and I follow blogs and podcasts that focus on the empowerment of the creator and a positive growth mindset, which I share on Twitter @thecreativepenn.

Choose the groups that work for the direction you want to take, and curate the voices you hear.

If you're in a group where people are negative and tear you down, then find another one. There are plenty of wonderful, supportive groups full of empowered creatives with an abundance mindset making money with their writing. You will find your tribe, it just might take a little time.

(6) Plan the transition to writing full time — if you want to make that shift

You certainly don't need to be a full-time writer to make money from your words, and in fact, many people enjoy their jobs and write as a side hustle. This takes the pressure off making an income with your art.

But if you want to go full time, as I did over a decade ago, then it can be done. But remember, it's more of a slow growth curve than an immediate shift.

I started writing in 2006 and it took me five years of building my author business on the side before I could leave my day job in 2011. We also sold our house, downsized and paid off all our debts as well as saving six months' income in case I didn't make any money at all. It took another four years before my writing business income exceeded my old day job.

If you want to follow the same path, start by planning to replace 10% of your monthly income with writing. Write down what that is for you.

Now do some sums.

If you can make $3 profit from the sale of a self-published book, how many books do you need to sell in a month to meet your target? It will be difficult if you only have one book, but what if you have five books? What if you add some of the other streams of income covered in this book?

Once you're making 10%, then you can decide on your next step. You can find more detail on taking your author career to the next level in *Your Author Business Plan*.

Over the years since I went full time, I have repeated the same pattern: I write and edit my words, I continue to learn about the craft and creative business — and importantly; I put that knowledge into action. I've made a lot of mistakes, but I keep moving forward. I love my creative career and if you want to take this path, it's definitely possible.

As historical fiction author Kristin Gleeson says, "Approach it like a business but with joy."

Questions:

- Do you want to make a living with your writing? Or make some money on the side of your day job? What are your reasons for this?

- Which areas spark the most ideas? What are you curious and/or enthusiastic about trying?

- What will you focus on first?

- What suits you as a creative personality?

- Who are your role models? What specifically do you want to model from them? Or how will you find a role model, if you don't have one yet?

- Why is skiing a good metaphor for making a living with your writing?

- If you're not already making any money from your writing, how will you make that first ten dollars?

- Have you set a deadline and written it down so you can see it every day?

- How much do you want this?

- If you've started to make some money, how can you expand your streams of income even further?

- Do you have a supportive community of writers who you learn from and can encourage and help you along the way? If not, how can you find them?

- What is 10% of your monthly income? How could you make that from your writing?

- How could you take the next step in the transition to making a living with your writing?

Resources:

- *Your Author Business Plan: Take Your Author Career to the Next Level* — Joanna Penn

- *Range: Why Generalists Triumph in a Specialized World* — David Epstein

- Consolidated question list in Appendix 3 and download — TheCreativePenn.com/makealivingdownload

- Companion print workbook with all the questions — www.TheCreativePenn.com/makealivingworkbook

Conclusion

We really are living in the best time in history to make a living with your writing and I hope you've found ideas in this book that will help you on the journey.

But of course, it's not all about the money.

It's about living a fulfilling creative life.

The global pandemic brought us face to face with our mortality. Life really is short. How will you spend the precious and limited time you have left?

I still remember the day I chose to follow this path. I stood in Anzac Square in downtown Brisbane, Australia, where I worked back then, tears streaming down my cheeks. I hated my job, and the years were flying by with nothing to show for them. Everything I did disappeared and ultimately, I was just another cog in the corporate wheel working to build someone else's company. I could pay the bills, but my creative spirit was withered and dying.

I changed direction and started writing seriously, taking courses, reading books, publishing my work, reaching readers, investing in building assets. It took years, but after more than a decade as a full-time author entrepreneur, I now measure my life by what I create.

Yes, I love making a great living on my own terms, but ultimately, I focus on creating a body of work I'm proud of through my books and my podcasts. Every day is another chance for my words to educate, inspire or entertain and my job now is meaningful as well as rewarding. This path is certainly possible for you, too.

You are a writer.

You can be an empowered creator and turn your words into multiple streams of income.

You just need to take the next step.

Need more help?

Sign up for my *free* Author Blueprint and email series, and receive useful information on writing, publishing, book marketing, and making a living with your writing:

www.TheCreativePenn.com/blueprint

* * *

Love podcasts?

Join me every Monday for The Creative Penn Podcast where I talk about writing, publishing, book marketing and the author business.

Available on your favorite podcast app.

Find the backlist episodes at

www.TheCreativePenn.com/podcast

Appendix 1:
Resources by Chapter

You can download this list at:

TheCreativePenn.com/makealivingdownload

First principles

- *The Successful Author Mindset: A Handbook for Surviving the Writer's Journey* — Joanna Penn

- *Mindset: Changing the Way You Think to Fulfil Your Potential* — Dr Carol Dweck

- *Your Author Business Plan: Take Your Author Career to the Next Level* — Joanna Penn

- List of useful money books and podcasts — www.TheCreativePenn.com/moneybooks

- Yaro Starak's Blog Profits Blueprint, regularly updated with best practices for making a living online — www.TheCreativePenn.com/BlogBlueprint

- Interview with Yaro Starak on freedom and long-term thinking — www.TheCreativePenn.com/yarofreedom

- Author Blueprint — www.TheCreativePenn.com/blueprint

- Authors Guild Report on author earnings — www.authorsguild.org/industry-advocacy/six-takeaways-from-the-authors-guild-2018-authors-income-survey/

- UK Authors' Earnings and Contracts 2018 — www.create.ac.uk/blog/2019/05/02/uk-authors-earnings-and-contracts-2018-a-survey-of-50000-writers/

- Books for writers by Kristine Kathryn Rusch and Dean Wesley Smith — www.wmgpublishinginc.com/writers

Part 1: How to Make Money with Books

1.1 Your publishing options and how the industry has changed

- *Free To Make: How the Maker Movement is Changing our Schools, Our Jobs and Our Minds* — Dale Dougherty

- *Makers: The New Industrial Revolution* — Chris Anderson

- Writer's Ink Podcast with hybrid author J.D. Barker and indie authors J. Thorn and Zach Bohannon. Conversations with traditional and indie authors around the publishing industry — WritersInkPodcast.com

- *The Book Business: What Everyone Needs to Know* — Mike Shatzkin and Robert Paris Riger

- *US Publishers, Authors, Booksellers Call Out Amazon's 'Concentrated Power' in the Market,* Publishing

Perspectives, August 2020 —
*www.publishingperspectives.com/2020/08/
us-publishers-authors-booksellers-call-out-amazons-
concentrated-power-in-the-book-market*

- *How COVID-19 has pushed companies over the
technology tipping point—and transformed business
forever*, McKinsey & Company —
*www.mckinsey.com/business-functions/strategy-and-
corporate-finance/our-insights/how-covid-19-has-
pushed-companies-over-the-technology-tipping-
point-and-transformed-business-forever*

1.2 Your book is a valuable intellectual property asset

- *The Copyright Handbook: What Every Writer Needs
To Know* — Stephen Fishman

- *Rethinking The Writing Business* —
Kristine Kathryn Rusch

- *Creative Self-Publishing: Make and Sell Your Books
Your Way* — Orna A. Ross

- *Selective Rights Licensing: Sell Your Book Rights At
Home and Abroad* —
Orna A. Ross and Helen Sedwick

- *The Magic Bakery: Copyright in the Modern World
of Fiction Publishing* — Dean Wesley Smith

- *Closing the Deal … on Your Terms: Agents, Contracts
and Other Considerations* —
Kristine Kathryn Rusch

- *Hollywood vs. The Author* —
Edited by Stephen Jay Schwartz

- Empowering authors around copyright. Interview with Rebecca Giblin — TheCreativePenn.com/rebeccagiblin

- The importance of editing and why authors need to understand their publishing contracts with Ruth Ware — www.TheCreativePenn.com/ruthware

- Society of Authors (UK) — SocietyOfAuthors.org

- The Authors Guild (USA) — AuthorsGuild.org

- Alliance of Independent Authors (global) — AllianceIndependentAuthors.org

- *How JK Rowling built a $25bn business*, Financial Times, June 2017 — www.ft.com/content/a24a70a6-55a9-11e7-9fed-c19e2700005f

- Brandon Sanderson's Kickstarter for the 10th anniversary leather-bound special edition of *The Way of Kings* — www.kickstarter.com/projects/dragonsteel/the-way-of-kings-10th-anniversary-leatherbound-edition

1.3 Traditional publishing

- *21 Insights for 21st Century Creatives* — Mark McGuinness

- *Closing the Deal ... on Your Terms: Agents, Contracts and Other Considerations* — Kristine Katherine Rusch

- *Selective Rights Licensing: Sell Your Book Rights At Home and Abroad* — Orna A. Ross and Helen Sedwick

- *Creative Self-Publishing: Make and Sell Your Books Your Way* — Orna A. Ross and the Alliance of Independent Authors

- *The Book Business: What Everyone Needs to Know* — Mike Shatzkin and Robert Paris Riger

- *Writers' and Artists' Yearbook* — Published annually by Bloomsbury in the UK. Listing of agents, publishers, awards and much more within the traditional publishing industry. They also have an online portal www.writersandartists.co.uk

- #PublishingPaidMe list of advances — TheCreativePenn.com/publishingpaidme

- Writer's Ink Podcast with hybrid author J.D. Barker and indie authors J. Thorn and Zach Bohannon. Conversations with traditional and indie authors around the publishing industry — WritersInkPodcast.com

- How publishing has changed, the importance of reading your contracts, changing pen names and more with psychological thriller author, Ruth Ware — TheCreativePenn.com/ruthware

- How to find and pitch a literary agent. Interview with Barbara Poelle — TheCreativePenn.com/barbarapoelle

- The Authors Guild (US) — AuthorsGuild.org

- Society of Authors (UK) — SocietyOfAuthors.org

- Alliance of Independent Authors — TheCreativePenn.com/alliance

- CREATe UK Authors' Earnings and Contracts 2018: A Survey of 50,000 Writers — Create.ac.uk/uk-authors-earnings-and-contracts-2018-a-survey-of-50000-writers

- *Koontz Inks Multibook Deal with Amazon Publishing*, Publishers Weekly, July 22, 2019 — www.publishersweekly.com/pw/by-topic/industry-news/book-deals/article/80740-koontz-inks-multibook-deal-with-amazon-publishing.html

- *A Year for the (Record) Books in Publishing*, Publishers Weekly, Jan 29, 2021 — www.publishersweekly.com/pw/by-topic/industry-news/bookselling/article/85453-a-year-for-the-record-books.html

- *How do authors earn a living? It's a Catch-22 situation*, Financial Times, June 7, 2019 — www.ft.com/content/5c7c31b8-82e3-11e9-a7f0-77d3101896ec

1.4 Self-publishing or becoming an indie author

- *Back yourself to write a book*, Alastair Humphreys — https://alastairhumphreys.com/back-yourself-to-write-a-book

- *A publisher of one's own: Virginia and Leonard Woolf and the Hogarth Press*, The Guardian, 24 April, 2017 — www.theguardian.com/books/2017/apr/24/a-publisher-of-ones-own-virginia-and-leonard-woolf-and-the-hogarth-press

- *Flower and questions*, with details on the money side of traditional vs. indie publishing, Ilona Andrews' blog — www.ilona-andrews.com/2021/flowers-and-questions

- *Money Can't Buy Happiness*, American Psychological Association, June 2011 — https://www.apa.org/news/press/releases/2011/06/buy-happiness

- Open Up to Indie Authors Campaign — www.allianceindependentauthors.org/open-up-campaign/

- *Successful Self-Publishing: How to Self-Publish and Market Your Book* — Joanna Penn

- *Your Author Business Plan: Take Your Author Career to the Next Level* — Joanna Penn

- *Creative Self-Publishing: Make and Sell Your Books Your Way* — Orna A. Ross and the Alliance of Independent Authors

- *An Author's Guide to Working with Libraries and Bookstores* — Mark Leslie Lefebvre

- *Winning Shelf Space: How to Get Your Self-Published Book into Bookstores* — Debbie Young, Orna A. Ross, and the Alliance of Independent Authors

- *Choose the Best Self-Publishing Services: ALLi's Guide to Assembling Your Tools and Your Team* — John Doppler and the Alliance of Independent Authors

- *Wide for the Win: Strategies to Sell Globally via Multiple Platforms and Forge Your Own Path to Success* — Mark Leslie Lefebvre

- WMG Writer's Guides by Dean Wesley Smith and Kristine Kathryn Rusch — WMGPublishinginc.com/writers

- Downloadable chart with spectrum of publishing possibilities by Jane Friedman — TheCreativePenn.com/publishingpaths

- List of editors — TheCreativePenn.com/editors

- List of book cover designers — TheCreativePenn.com/bookcoverdesign

- List of formatting options — TheCreativePenn.com/formatting

- List of useful tools — TheCreativePenn.com/tools

- Alliance of Independent Authors Watchdog listing — SelfPublishingAdvice.org/best-self-publishing-services

- Alliance of Independent Authors — AllianceIndependentAuthors.org

- Alliance of Independent Authors blog and podcast — SelfPublishingAdvice.org

- Mark Dawson's Self-Publishing Formula 101 Course — www.TheCreativePenn.com/101

- Wide for the Win Facebook group — Facebook.com/groups/wideforthewin

- 20BooksTo50K Facebook group — Facebook.com/groups/20Booksto50k

1.5 Write more books

- *Productivity for Authors: Find Time to Write, Organize Your Author Life, and Decide What Really Matters* — Joanna Penn

- *How To Write Non-Fiction: Turn Your Knowledge into Words* — Joanna Penn

- *Playing the Short Game: How to Market and Sell Short Fiction* — Douglas Smith

- *Taking the Short Tack: Creating Income and Connecting with Readers Using Short Fiction* — Matty Dalrymple

- *Co-writing a Book: Collaboration and Co-creation for Writers* — Joanna Penn and J. Thorn

- WMG Writer's Guides by Dean Wesley Smith and Kristine Kathryn Rusch — WMGPublishinginc.com/writers

- Scrivener software for writing — www.TheCreativePenn.com/scrivenersoftware

- ProWritingAid for editing — www.TheCreativePenn.com/prowritingaid

- Resources and interviews on dictation — www.TheCreativePenn.com/dictation

- Interview with prolific fantasy author Lindsay Buroker on writing a series — www.TheCreativePenn.com/writeseries

- Interview on making money with short fiction with award-winning author Douglas Smith — TheCreativePenn.com/shortfiction

1.6 Write books that people want to buy

- Publisher Rocket for keywords and categories — www.TheCreativePenn.com/rocket

- Free tutorial on researching keywords — TheCreativePenn.com/rocketkeywords

- Genre and category research reports at K-lytics — TheCreativePenn.com/genre

- *Write To Market: Deliver a Book That Sells* —
  Chris Fox

1.7 Publish in multiple formats

- *Successful Self-Publishing: How to Self-Publish and Market Your Book* — Joanna Penn

- Curl Up Press, Books you want to stay in for — www.CurlUpPress.com

- *Creative Self-Publishing: Make and Sell Your Books Your Way* — Orna A. Ross and the Alliance of Independent Authors

- *An Author's Guide to Working with Libraries & Bookstores* — Mark Leslie Lefebvre

- *Audio for Authors: Audiobooks, Podcasting, and Voice Technologies* — Joanna Penn

- *How to Make Real Money Selling Books without Worrying about Returns* — Brian Jud

- *How to Get Your Book Into Schools and Double Your Income With Volume Sales* —
  David H. Hendrickson

- Formatting options including software and free-lancers — www.TheCreativePenn.com/formatting

- Vellum software for ebook and print formatting — www.TheCreativePenn.com/vellum

- Tutorial on how to use Vellum for formatting — www.TheCreativePenn.com/vellum-tutorial

- Interview with David Chilton on bulk sales — www.TheCreativePenn.com/davidchilton

- David Chilton's course on bulk sales — www.TheCreativePenn.com/bulksales

- Interview with David Hendrickson on selling directly into schools — www.TheCreativePenn.com/schoolsales

- Companion Workbook for How to Make a Living with your Writing Third Edition — TheCreativePenn.com/makealivingworkbook

- *No, Crowdfunding is not begging*, Self Publishing Advice, May 2015 — www.selfpublishingadvice. org/crowdfunding-is-not-begging

- Brandon Sanderson's Kickstarter for the 10th anniversary leather-bound special edition of *The Way of Kings* — www.kickstarter.com/projects/dragonsteel/ the-way-of-kings-10th-anniversary-leatherbound- edition

1.8 Publish globally

- My Kobo Writing Life map — www.TheCreativePenn.com/kobomap

- *The Top Ten Publishing Trends Every Author Needs to Know in 2021*, Written Word Media, 7 Jan 2021 — www.writtenwordmedia.com/the-top-ten- publishing-trends-every-author-needs-to-know- in-2021

- *Selective Rights Licensing: Sell your Book Rights at Home and Abroad* — Orna Ross and Helen Sedwick

- *An Author's Guide to Working with Libraries and Bookstores* — Mark Leslie Lefebvre

- *Wide for the Win: Strategies to Sell Globally via Multiple Platforms and Forge Your Own Path to Success* — Mark Leslie Lefebvre

- Self-publishing in Translation: Adventures with AI and German — TheCreativePenn.com/AIGerman

- AI translation service — www.deepl.com

- Interview with Karen Inglis on her success with children's books — SelfPublishingFormula.com/episode-239

- Ultimate Guide to Rights Licensing from the Alliance of Independent Authors — SelfPublishing-Advice.org/rights-licensing-for-indie-authors

- International Association of Professional Translators and Interpreters — www.iapti.org

- Institute of Translation and Interpreting — www.iti.org.uk

- Reedsy Marketplace for translators — www.TheCreativePenn.com/reedsy

- Reedsy free course on international pricing — www.TheCreativePenn.com/internationalpricing

1.9 Sell direct to your audience

- ALLi Campaign: Self-Publishing 3.0: How and Why Indie Authors Should Sell Direct to Readers — and What ALLi is Doing to Help, Self Publishing Advice, 4 June, 2018 — www.selfpublishingadvice.org/self-publishing-3-0-indie-authors-selling-direct

- Payhip for selling ebooks and audiobooks direct — www.TheCreativePenn.com/payhip

- Buy ebooks and audiobooks directly from me — www.Payhip.com/thecreativepenn

- Process of using a Payhip coupon — www.TheCreativePenn.com/payhip-coupon

- Bookfunnel for delivery of ebooks and audiobooks — www.TheCreativePenn.com/bookfunnel

- My tutorial on selling ebooks and audiobooks direct with Payhip and Bookfunnel — www.TheCreativePenn.com/selldirecttutorial

- The Ultimate Guide to Selling Books on your Author Website by the Alliance of Independent Authors — SelfPublishingAdvice.org/selling-books-on-your-author-website

- Enabled Works: Contract packing, fulfilment, and storage specialists — www.enabledworks.co.uk

- Aerio, Ingram site for selling direct — www.aer.io

- US and UK site for book sales that benefit independent booksellers — bookshop.org

1.10 Market your books

- *How to Market a Book* — Joanna Penn

- *Strangers to Superfans: A Marketing Guide to the Reader Journey* — David Gaughran

- *How to Market a Book: Over-perform in a Crowded Market* — Ricardo Fayet

- My author website tutorial — www.TheCreativePenn.com/authorwebsite

- My email list set-up tutorial —
www.TheCreativePenn.com/setup-email-list

- 101 Course for Authors by Mark Dawson, including
the basics you need in place for successful self-
publishing — www.TheCreativePenn.com/101

- Ads for Authors course by Mark Dawson, including
Facebook, Amazon, and BookBub Ads —
www.TheCreativePenn.com/ads

- Your First 10K Readers course by Nick Stephenson
— www.TheCreativePenn.com/10k

- Free thriller — www.JFPenn.com/free

- Free Author Blueprint —
www.TheCreativePenn.com/blueprint

- Reedsy Marketplace for free courses on marketing
and professionals if you want to outsource marketing — www.TheCreativePenn.com/reedsy

Part 2: How to Make Money with your Writing in Other Ways

2.1 Your author ecosystem

- *Your Author Business Plan: Take Your Author Career
to the Next Level* — Joanna Penn

2.2 Affiliate income

- Smart Passive Income Guide to Ethical Affiliate
Marketing — SmartPassiveIncome.com/guide/
affiliate-marketing-strategies

- Amazon Associates — affiliate-program.amazon.com

- Apple's affiliate program — affiliate.itunes.apple.com/resources

- Rakuten affiliate for Kobo — rakutenadvertising.com/en-uk/affiliate

- Bookshop.org affiliate program — www.bookshop.org/affiliates/profile/introduction

- Sites for creating multi-links — Booklinker.net and Books2Read.com

- Pretty Links for WordPress to create easy to manage affiliate links — PrettyLinks.com

- List of editors — TheCreativePenn.com/editors

- List of book cover designers — TheCreativePenn.com/bookcoverdesign

- Tools for writing, editing, publishing, and marketing —TheCreativePenn.com/tools

- Online courses for writers — TheCreativePenn.com/courses

- Tutorial on how to set up your author website and email list — TheCreativePenn.com/authorwebsite

- Tutorial on how to format your ebook and print book using Vellum at TheCreativePenn.com/vellum-tutorial

- How to find and work with professional editors — www.TheCreativePenn.com/how-to-find-and-work-with-professional-editors

- Webinar replay on how to automate your author marketing — TheCreativePenn.com/nickjo

2.3 Crowdfunding, patronage and subscription

- Kickstarter Creator Handbook — kickstarter.com/help/handbook

- Kickstarter Publishing and Journalism projects — Kickstarter.com/publishing

- Kickstarter projects by Dean Wesley Smith and Kristine Kathryn Rusch — www.kickstarter.com/profile/403649867/created

- Brandon Sanderson Way of Kings Kickstarter project — Kickstarter.com/projects/dragonsteel/the-way-of-kings-10th-anniversary-leatherbound-edition

- Kickstarter best practices course from WMG Publishing — wmg-publishing-workshops-and-lectures.teachable.com/p/kickstarter

- Patreon Creator Help — support.patreon.com

- YouTube Creator Academy — Creatoracademy.youtube.com/page/course/channel-memberships

- Facebook Fan Subscriptions — Facebook.com/creators/getting-started-with-fan-subscriptions

- The Hotsheet publishing email from Jane Friedman — hotsheetpub.com

- Substack for paid email newsletters — Substack.com

- Fan-supported tips — Ko-fi.com and BuyMeACoffee.com

- ConvertKit Commerce for recurring subscriptions — TheCreativePenn.com/convert

- 1000 True Fans, Kevin Kelly — www.kk.org/thetechnium/1000-true-fans

- T. Thorn Coyle Substack email newsletter — www.tthorncoyle.substack.com

- Patreon non-fiction articles on business and publishing by Kristine Kathryn Rusch — www.Patreon.com/kristinekathrynrusch

- Patreon science fiction and fantasy novels by Lindsay Buroker — www.Patreon.com/lindsayburoker

- Patreon fiction and poetry with Orna Ross — www.Patreon.com/ornaross

- Patreon short stories and poetry with Seanan McGuire — www.Patreon.com/seananmcguire

- Patreon community for Black and POC (Person of Color) writers — www.Patreon.com/wellreadblackgirl

- Patreon for The Creative Penn Podcast — www.Patreon.com/thecreativepenn

- Patreon for the Stark Reflections on Writing and Publishing Podcast with Mark Leslie Lefebvre — www.Patreon.com/starkreflections

- Patrons for the Writers Ink Podcast with J. Thorn, J.D. Barker, and Zach Bohannon — www.Patreon.com/writersinkpodcast

2.4 Professional speaking, teaching, performing, and live events

- *Public Speaking for Authors, Creatives and Other Introverts* — Joanna Penn

- The Society of Authors (UK) guidance on rates and fees: Societyofauthors.org/advice/rates-fees

- My speaking page — www.TheCreativePenn.com/speaking

- Toastmasters — www.toastmasters.org

- National Speakers Association USA — www.nsaspeaker.org

- Professional Speaking Association UK — www.thepsa.co.uk

- Global Speakers Federation with links to other country-specific sites — www.GlobalSpeakersFederation.net

2.5 Online courses, webinars, events, and membership sites

- Teachable for creating and selling online courses — TheCreativePenn.com/teachable

- My courses including on how to Turn What You Know Into An Online Course — www.TheCreativePenn.com/learn

- Masterclass courses by famous authors, writers, screenwriters and more — TheCreativePenn.com/masterclass

2.6 Advertising and sponsorship

- Interview with Meg La Torre on her multiple streams of income based on her iWriterly YouTube channel: TheCreativePenn.com/youtubeincome

- My YouTube channel — www.YouTube.com/thecreativepenn

- iWriterly YouTube channel — www.youtube.com/iwriterly

- Jenna Moreci's YouTube channel — www.youtube.com/jennamoreci

- Midroll podcast advertising — www.Midroll.com

2.7 Physical products and merchandise

- *Merchandise for Authors: Engage Your Readers While Increasing Your Income* — Melissa Addey

- *Rethinking The Writing Business* — Kristine Kathryn Rusch

- Print-on-demand merchandise sites — Redbubble.com, Teespring.com, Zazzle.com, and Society6.com

- My Society 6 store — www.Society6.com/creativepenn

- XKCD for cartoons and products — www.XKCD.com

- Romance author J.A. Huss merchandise — www.Society6.com/jahuss

- Kimberley Ward custom jewelry — www.etsy.com/uk/shop/WardsWhimsicalWorks

- Campaign Coins — www.campaigncoins.com

2.8 Freelance writing and ghostwriting

- 71 ways to make money as a freelance writer. Guide from The Write Life on paying freelance opportunities with specific rates, as well as the practical information, including how to pitch, land clients, set rates and create invoices — www.TheCreativePenn.com/freelance

- TheWriteLife.com — Helping writers create, connect and earn with articles and resources for freelancers

- MakeALivingWriting.com — Six-figure freelancer Carol Tice has been helping freelance writers for almost a decade. The site provides resources, articles and books to help freelance writers make money.

- ProWritingAid for editing — www.TheCreativePenn.com/prowritingaid

- Grammarly for editing — www.TheCreativePenn.com/grammarly

2.9 Consulting or coaching

- Teachable Coaching platform — TheCreativePenn.com/teachable

- Bestselling UK crime writers offering coaching and editing — CrimeFictionCoach.com

- The Author Success Mastermind, small group coaching with J. Thorn — www.TheAuthorSuccessMastermind.com

- Creative coach Mark McGuinness — www.LateralAction.com/coaching

2.10 Author services

- Alliance of Independent Authors for Partner Membership — www.AllianceIndependentAuthors.org/partnership-approval

- Reedsy marketplace for vetted professionals: www.TheCreativePenn.com/reedsy

- List of editors — www.TheCreativePenn.com/editors

- List of book cover designers — www.TheCreativePenn.com/bookcoverdesign

- List of formatters — www.TheCreativePenn.com/formatting

2.11 Other ways to make money with your writing

- The Society of Authors list of grants — SocietyOfAuthors.org/Grants

- FundsForWriters list of grants — FundsForWriters.com/grants

- Authors Guild list of contests, grants, and residences — AuthorsGuild.org/category/contests-grants

- Arts Council UK grants — Artscouncil.org.uk/projectgrants

- PLR for UK and Ireland — www.plr.uk.com

- ALCS for UK — www.alcs.co.uk

- PLR for Canada — PublicLendingRight.ca

- List of countries with PLR schemes — plrinternational.com/established

- Wattpad information for writers — www.wattpad.com/writers

- Alliance of Independent Authors list of awards and contests — www.SelfPublishingAdvice.org/author-awards-contests-rated-reviewed

- List of book and novel-writing competitions — www.christopherfielden.com/short-story-tips-and-writing-advice/book-and-novel-competitions.php

- List of short story competitions and awards — www.christopherfielden.com/short-story-tips-and-writing-advice/short-story-competitions.php

The transition to making a living with your writing

- *Your Author Business Plan: Take Your Author Career to the Next Level* — Joanna Penn

- *Range: Why Generalists Triumph in a Specialized World* — David Epstein

- Consolidated question list in Appendix 3 and download — TheCreativePenn.com/makealivingdownload

- Companion print workbook with all the questions — www.TheCreativePenn.com/makealivingworkbook

Appendix 2: Bibliography

You can download this list at:

TheCreativePenn.com/makealivingdownload

21 Insights for 21st Century Creatives —
Mark McGuinness

*An Author's Guide to Working with Libraries
and Bookstores* — Mark Leslie Lefebvre

*Audio for Authors: Audiobooks, Podcasting, and Voice
Technologies* — Joanna Penn

*Choose the Best Self-Publishing Services: ALLi's Guide to
Assembling Your Tools and Your Team* —
John Doppler and the Alliance of Independent Authors

*Closing the Deal ... on Your Terms: Agents, Contracts and
Other Considerations* — Kristine Katherine Rusch

*Co-writing a Book: Collaboration and Co-creation for
Writers* — Joanna Penn and J. Thorn

*Creative Self-Publishing: Make and Sell Your Books Your
Way* — Orna A. Ross

*Free To Make: How the Maker Movement is Changing our
Schools, Our Jobs and Our Minds* — Dale Dougherty

Hollywood vs. The Author —
Edited by Stephen Jay Schwartz

How to Get Your Book Into Schools and Double Your Income With Volume Sales — David H. Hendrickson

How to Market a Book — Joanna Penn

How to Market a Book: Over-perform in a Crowded Market — Ricardo Fayet

How to Make Real Money Selling Books without Worrying about Returns — Brian Jud

How To Write Non-Fiction: Turn Your Knowledge into Words — Joanna Penn

Look Both Ways: Illustrated Essays on the Intersection of Life and Design — Debbie Millman

Makers: The New Industrial Revolution — Chris Anderson

Mindset: Changing the Way You Think to Fulfil Your Potential — Dr Carol Dweck

Playing the Short Game: How to Market and Sell Short Fiction — Douglas Smith

Productivity for Authors: Find Time to Write, Organize Your Author Life, and Decide What Really Matters — Joanna Penn

Public Speaking for Authors, Creatives and Other Introverts — Joanna Penn

Rethinking The Writing Business — Kristine Kathryn Rusch

Selective Rights Licensing: Sell Your Book Rights At Home and Abroad — Orna A. Ross and Helen Sedwick

Strangers to Superfans: A Marketing Guide to the Reader Journey — David Gaughran

Successful Self-Publishing: How to Self-Publish and Market Your Book — Joanna Penn

Taking the Short Tack: Creating Income and Connecting with Readers Using Short Fiction — Matty Dalrymple

The Book Business: What Everyone Needs to Know — Mike Shatzkin and Robert Paris Riger

The Copyright Handbook: What Every Writer Needs To Know — Stephen Fishman

The Magic Bakery: Copyright in the Modern World of Fiction Publishing — Dean Wesley Smith

The Successful Author Mindset: A Handbook for Surviving the Writer's Journey — Joanna Penn

Wide for the Win: Strategies to Sell Globally via Multiple Platforms and Forge Your Own Path to Success — Mark Leslie Lefebvre

Winning Shelf Space: How to Get Your Self-Published Book into Bookstores — Debbie Young, Orna A. Ross, and the Alliance of Independent Authors

Write To Market: Deliver a Book That Sells — Chris Fox

Writers' and Artists' Yearbook — Published annually by Bloomsbury in the UK

Your Author Business Plan: Take Your Author Career to the Next Level — Joanna Penn

Appendix 3:
List of Questions

You can download this list at:

TheCreativePenn.com/makealivingdownload

First principles

- What is your definition of success?

- What will you do to achieve it?

- How much money is a 'living' for you? How much money do you want to make per year from your writing?

- Why are multiple streams of income important over the long term?

- Do you believe you can make a living with your writing? Do you need to work on your money mindset?

- How much of your income is money for time? How much is scalable? How could you shift this split?

- Writing is only one aspect of making a living with your writing. What are some other things you might need to learn?

- How will you embrace the growth mindset?

- Who are your models? How do they make money?

Are those methods possible for you?

- If you don't have models in mind yet, how could you find them?

- Why is it important to think long term about making a living with your writing?

Part 1: How to Make Money with Books

1.1 Your publishing options and how the industry has changed

- What are the opportunities for your book/s if you consider the market to be global, digital, and mobile?

- What are some shifts to digital business that you've seen or read about due to the pandemic?

- How has your own reading and purchasing behavior changed over the last decade?

- How do you currently support independent creators in the way you choose to purchase?

- How could you embrace the Maker Movement as part of your own creative journey?

- Do you consider yourself an empowered creator? How could you move further toward this in order to expand your creative potential?

1.2 Your book is a valuable intellectual property asset

- What is copyright?

- How does rights licensing make you money?

- Why is selective rights licensing a good idea?

- How can you empower yourself with the knowledge you need in this area?

1.3 Traditional publishing

- What are the benefits of traditional publishing?

- What are the downsides of traditional publishing?

- How does the money work?

- Are you considering this route to publication? What are your reasons for this? What is your definition of success?

- How could you take the next step?

Contracts are for negotiation, so discuss the following with your agent and/or publisher:

- What countries or territories will the book be published in? If it won't be available everywhere, then why license World English?

- What formats are specified? For example, if audiobook rights are included, how long will it be before the audiobook is published and in which territories?

- What subsidiary rights are included, and how will these be exploited? Many publishers will sub-license foreign languages or may license for film/TV and other media.

- How long is the contract for? Is it term-limited, for example, five years for foreign language rights? When and how will the rights revert? For example, if the audiobook is not produced within three years, the rights revert to the author.

- Is there a 'do not compete' clause which may prevent you publishing during the term of the contract under the same name, in the same world or with the same characters?

1.4 Self-publishing or becoming an indie author

- What's the difference between self-publishing and becoming an indie author?

- What are the benefits of being an indie author?

- What are the downsides?

- How does the money work?

- Are you considering this route to publication? What are your reasons? What is your definition of success?

- How will you find recommended freelancers and services to work with?

- What do you need to take the next step?

1.5 Write more books

- How could you write and produce more books?
- What is stopping you from writing more books?
- How can you break through those blocks?

1.6 Write books that people want to buy

- How can you make sure that there is an audience for your book?
- Who are your 'comp' authors and/or specific books?
- What are the reader expectations for these types of books?
- What do the top-selling books have in common? How does your book fit alongside them?
- What sub-categories are they in?
- What keywords might be relevant?
- How could you combine writing what you love with writing what people want to buy?

1.7 Publish in multiple formats

- What formats do you read?
- What formats are your books available in right now?
- What other formats could you create? (If you retain the rights)

1.8 Publish globally

- Are your books available globally in English in ebook, paperback, and audiobook (if appropriate)?

- How can you expand your distribution to more global markets?

- Are you interested in foreign rights licensing? Would self-publishing in translation work for your author business?

- What are your next steps to take this further?

- How could you market your books to a global audience?

1.9 Sell direct to your audience

- What are the benefits of selling direct, both for the customer and for you?

- How could you sell direct from your website?

- What do you need to have in place to make this worthwhile? If you're not at that point yet, how can you move in that direction?

1.10 Market your books

- What is your current attitude to book marketing? How could you improve your mindset?

- If you have a book or more out already, do you have the basics in place?

- How could you use your books to market your books?

- What kinds of marketing are you interested in learning more about? What might work for your personality and lifestyle over the long term?

- How could you improve your marketing skills?

- When is a good time to outsource your marketing? Is it the right time for you?

Part 2: How to Make Money with your Writing in Other Ways

2.1 Your author ecosystem

- How does an ecosystem work to drive revenue in multiple ways?

- What does your ecosystem look like now?

- If you carry on as you are for the next five years, or ten years, what will your ecosystem look like?

- What do you need to change to ensure it works for you over the long term?

2.2 Affiliate income

- What are the pros and cons of affiliate income?

- How can you be an ethical and successful affiliate?

- How could you start making affiliate income?

- How will you expand this to increase traffic and revenue?

2.3 Crowdfunding, patronage, and subscription

- What are the benefits of crowdfunding?

- Research the publishing and writing section of Kickstarter and Indiegogo to find ideas for what you could create. What sparks your curiosity?

- What are the benefits of patronage or ongoing subscription?

- Research the writing and creative section of Patreon to find examples of creators who make a monthly income. What might work for your community?

- How could you successfully incorporate crowdfunding and/or patronage into your streams of income? What do you need to have in place to make this happen?

2.4 Professional speaking, teaching, performing, and live events

- What are some benefits of speaking and how could you incorporate it as a stream of income?

- Research speakers in your niche. What can you learn from their websites around branding, pitching, products, and pricing?

- Who is your target market for professional speaking? How could you reach them? What rates do they pay?

- What topic/s could you speak on? Does this fit with your target market and your expectation of income?

- Do you need training and/or experience in order to charge for professional speaking? How will you develop these further?

2.5 Online courses, webinars, events, and membership sites

- What are the benefits of creating an online course? How could it form part of your multiple streams of income?

- What type of course might be useful to your audience?

- What topic will your course be on?

- How much time do you need to set aside for learning new skills, preparing and recording your course?

- What tools and technology do you need to investigate? What skills do you need to learn, and how could they be useful for your wider author business?

- What is stopping you from creating an online course?

2.6 Advertising and sponsorship

- Do you have a niche audience that is large enough to consider offering advertising or sponsorship?

- Which companies or services might work best for your audience?

2.7 Physical products and merchandise

- What are the pros and cons of physical products and merchandising? How do these differ from swag?

- What aspects of your books or business might be relevant for products and merchandising?

- What could you create through print-on-demand? What might need to be a bigger project with more funding?

- Do you have the right to use the images related to your books on merchandise?

2.8 Freelance writing and ghostwriting

- What are the pros and cons of freelance writing and/ or ghostwriting?

- How could you develop this stream of income for your author business?

2.9 Consulting or coaching

- What are the pros and cons of offering consulting or coaching services?

- What could you help people with?

- Who are the successful coaches and consultants in your niche? What can you learn from them and model in order to set up and grow your own service?

2.10 Author services

- Do you want to offer services to authors? What would be the best fit for your skills, and what does the author community need?

- How will you balance your time between clients and your own creative work?

2.11 Other ways to make money with your writing

- Do any of these additional ideas spark your curiosity? How could you take the next step?

The transition to making a living with your writing

- Do you want to make a living with your writing? Or make some money on the side of your day job? What are your reasons for this?

- Which areas spark the most ideas? What are you curious and/or enthusiastic about trying?

- What will you focus on first?

- What suits you as a creative personality?

- Who are your role models? What specifically do you want to model from them? Or how will you find a role model, if you don't have one yet?

- Why is skiing a good metaphor for making a living with your writing?

- If you're not already making any money from your writing, how will you make that first ten dollars?

- Have you set a deadline and written it down so you can see it every day?

- How much do you want this?

- If you've started to make some money, how can you expand your streams of income even further?

- Do you have a supportive community of writers who you learn from and can encourage and help you along the way? If not, how can you find them?

- What is 10% of your monthly income? How could you make that from your writing?

- How could you take the next step in the transition to making a living with your writing?

Appendix 4: Streams of Income Survey results

You can download this Appendix at:

TheCreativePenn.com/makealivingdownload

In January 2021, I sent out a survey on Author Streams of Income to my email list and shared it on my podcast and on social media.

It included a list of income streams with options to select multiple items and I asked for any others I might have forgotten, as well as tips for writers who wanted to pursue these opportunities.

738 writers responded.

94% make income from multiple streams.

6% of respondents had only one stream of writing income — either freelance writing, traditional publishing, or self-publishing ebooks only.

Summary of main income streams

Respondents could select multiple options on the list or add their own. This is the percentage of the total who selected each option.

84% — Self-publishing ebook sales

77% — Self-publishing print sales

36% — Selling books direct

27% — Self-publishing audiobook sales

26% — Teaching or speaking live or online

26% — Freelance writing and/or ghostwriting

23% — Traditional publishing advance and royalties

22% — Affiliate income

19% — Consulting and/or coaching

19% — Author services

12% — Online course sales

10% — Patronage e.g. Patreon

9% — Merchandise

6% — Licensing foreign rights

6% — Advertising revenue e.g. podcast or YouTube

3% — Licensing subsidiary rights e.g. film/TV options

2% — Crowdfunding e.g. Kickstarter

Thank you to everyone who responded to the survey. I read every comment and suggestion and while not every tip is quoted in the book, it's heartening to see so many income streams and ideas.

More Books And Courses From Joanna Penn

Non-Fiction Books for Authors

How to Write Non-Fiction

How to Market a Book

How to Make a Living with your Writing

Productivity for Authors

Successful Self-Publishing

Your Author Business Plan

The Successful Author Mindset

Public Speaking for Authors, Creatives
and Other Introverts

Audio for Authors:
Audiobooks, Podcasting, and Voice Technologies

The Healthy Writer

Business for Authors:
How to be an Author Entrepreneur

Co-writing a Book

Career Change

www.TheCreativePenn.com/books

Courses for authors

How to Write a Novel

How to Write Non-Fiction

Multiple Streams of Income from your Writing

Your Author Business Plan

Content Marketing for Fiction

Productivity for Authors

Turn What You Know Into An Online Course

Co-Writing a Book

www.TheCreativePenn.com/courses

Thriller novels as J.F. Penn

ARKANE Action-adventure Thrillers

Stone of Fire #1
Crypt of Bone #2
Ark of Blood #3
One Day In Budapest #4
Day of the Vikings #5
Gates of Hell #6
One Day in New York #7
Destroyer of Worlds #8
End of Days #9
Valley of Dry Bones #10
Tree of Life #11

Brooke and Daniel Crime Thrillers

Desecration #1
Delirium #2
Deviance #3

Mapwalker Dark Fantasy Trilogy

Map of Shadows #1
Map of Plagues #2
Map of the Impossible #3

Other Books and Short Stories

Risen Gods

A Thousand Fiendish Angels:
Short stories based on Dante's Inferno

The Dark Queen:
An Underwater Archaeology Short Story

More books coming soon.

You can sign up to be notified of new releases, giveaways
and pre-release specials - plus, get a free book!

www.JFPenn.com/free

About Joanna Penn

Joanna Penn writes non-fiction for authors and is an award-nominated, New York Times and USA Today bestselling thriller author as J.F. Penn. She's also an award-winning podcaster, creative entrepreneur, and international professional speaker.

She is an international professional speaker, podcaster, and award-winning entrepreneur. She lives in Bath, England with her husband and enjoys a nice G&T.

Joanna's award-winning site for writers, TheCreativePenn. com, helps people to write, publish and market their books through articles, audio, video and online products as well as live workshops.

Love thrillers? www.JFPenn.com

Love travel? Check out my Books and Travel podcast
www.BooksAndTravel.page

Connect with Joanna

www.TheCreativePenn.com
joanna@TheCreativePenn.com

www.twitter.com/thecreativepenn
www.facebook.com/TheCreativePenn
www.Instagram.com/jfpennauthor
www.youtube.com/thecreativepenn

Acknowledgments

Thanks to my community at The Creative Penn website and podcast. Your enthusiasm and support keeps me going!

Thanks as ever to Jane Dixon Smith for the cover design and print interior formatting, and to Liz Dexter at LibroEditing for proofreading, and Alexandra Amor for beta reading.

Thanks to the 738 writers who took my survey on streams of income. Thanks in particular to the authors quoted within the book: Sacha Black, Ariele Sieling, Angeline Trevena, Angie Scarr, J.D. Barker, Karen Inglis, Mark Dawson, Orna Ross, Mark McGuinness, Alastair Humphreys, Jeremy Bassetti, Natalie Keller Reinert, Kat Bellemore, Jessie Clever, Sadie King, Holly Worton, Nadine Mutas, Jo Parfitt, Jeff Elkins, T. Thorn Coyle, Peter Ball, Melissa Addey, Kimberley Ward, Joseph Lallo, Sarah Baxter, Elizabeth McCowan, Roz Morris, A.D. Starrling, Alexandra Amor, Courtney Kenney, Ann Thomson, Jessica Bell, Mark Leslie Lefebvre, Karen Lock Kolp, Susan E. Farriss, Jack and Kitty Norton, Sally Rose, Kaecey McCormick, Rachael Herron, Travis Senzaki, Clare Sager, and Kristin Gleeson.

Made in the USA
Middletown, DE
27 June 2022